through a widow's eyes

WHAT HAPPENS AFTER SUICIDE

Copyright ©2024
by Tammie Osborne
All rights reserved.

No part of this book may be used or reproduced by any means: graphic, electronic, or mechanical, including photocopying, recording, taping, or by any information storage retrieval system without the written permission of the author except in the case of brief quotations embodied in critical articles and reviews. Because of the dynamic nature of the Internet, any web addresses or links contained in this book may have changed since publication and may no longer be valid. Although every precaution has been taken to verify the accuracy of the information contained herein, the author and publisher assume no responsibility for any errors or omissions so that no liability is assumed for damages that may result from the use of the information contained within. The views expressed in this work are solely those of the author and do not necessarily reflect the views of the publisher whereby the publisher hereby disclaims any responsibility for them.
All photographs displayed in this book are
the personal property of the author.

Traitmarker Books

www.traitmarkerbooks.com
traitmarker@gmail.com
Cover Design: Robbie Grayson III

Paperback ISBN | 979-8-3302-5268-8

Through a Widow's Eyes
WHAT HAPPENS AFTER SUICIDE

TAMMIE **LIZANA**-OSBORNE

To My Robby, My First Love—

Losing you has opened my eyes and heart to a more extraordinary and purpose-filled life—a life that will lead me down many unknown roads. Some of my choices about which roads to take will end up hurting me, and I will be alone, frightened, and lost. But every wrong path I take will have its own deeper meaning. By navigating each, I shall find myself again and be healed. Though there's a lot I don't know, I do know that you're in Heaven and no longer suffering.

To Family and Friends—

To those of you who stopped your lives the week that Robby died so that I wouldn't have to be alone and to those of you who have so patiently loved me through the worst nightmare of my life, I am so rich because of every one of you. You have watched me stumble, get up, and fall over and over again, yet you're still with me. Your value to me is forever priceless.

To Readers—

For every one of you who picks up this book, I pray that you find your healing spot, recognize it, and cherish it so that you can move forward in life. Writing this book has helped me heal in a way that no other therapy has.

*You own everything that happened to you.
Tell your stories. If people wanted you to write
warmly about them, they should
have behaved better.*

—Anne Lamott

Contents

A Note from the Publisher | ix
Introduction: Through a Widow's Eyes | xi

1 | My Nightmare Begins 15
2 | Getting to Know Us 29
3 | Two Losses 41
4 | Young Love 53
5 | It's Complicated 67

>   ~Mommy Issues
>   ~Rekindled

6 | Blending Our Lives 87
7 | The Beginning of the End 109
8 | New Beginnings 125

Special Acknowledgments | 151
Questions for Book Discussion | 153
Photo Gallery | 163
About the Author | 169
Contact | 171

Love never fails.

—St. Paul

A Note
From the Publisher

The publisher is providing this book and its contents on an "as is" basis and makes no representations or warranties of any kind with respect to this book or its contents and disclaims all such representations and warranties, including but not limited to warranties of mental healthcare for a particular purpose.

The content of this book is for informational purposes only and is not intended to diagnose, treat, cure, or prevent any mental condition or disease. This book is not intended as a substitute for consultation with a licensed practitioner. Please consult with a physician or healthcare specialist regarding the suggestions and recommendations made in this book.

TRAITMARKER BOOKS
Robbie Grayson III | FRANKLIN, TN

INTRODUCTION
Through a Widow's Eyes

WHEN we marry, we profess our undying Love for another. We promise to love the other person through sickness and health until death do us part, no matter what, and forever, right? So, what happens when the one who promised you that your "forever together" would be in the hands of God chooses your "forever date" for you?

Do I run and hide? Am I supposed to die with him? Am I allowed to continue to live? Am I supposed to stop living life or live it just as we had planned together? Who can I trust? Who should make decisions for me during this new and ever-changing daily schedule? How long should I wait before I give my heart away again? And will that ever happen? Will I ever be comfortable with someone else enough to entrust my heart and soul to them?

And what about those left behind—the ones you thought loved you that resemble vultures more than loved ones? Do they really love me, or are they having a "moment" where coping with the loss looks like greed? How do I know who my true team is, and what do I do with those who aren't but won't go away? How can I risk having them around when I am trying to heal?

I had asked myself these questions thousands of times the first year since Robby left me. What I learned was that even though I was living the worst year of my life, I could not afford to entertain any negativity from myself or anyone else. More than any other strategy for protecting my sanity so I could find the strength to deal with everything now on my shoulders, I found this one to be the most critical.

Writing this book has served many purposes, but the main one is that it has helped me heal through the most horrific pain I have ever felt in my life. Because it helped me so much, I want to share what I learned with the reader. I want you to know that you aren't the only person whose life feels so desperately empty after going through your nightmare. I also want you to understand that a light will be at the end of your tunnel.

"Stake It" Sections

When experiencing heartache like this, you can't think about tomorrow, next week, or next month. It's enough to get through the day. That's why you will find a "Stake It" in every chapter that will anchor you to a decision you should be considering at that moment. Because Robby and I owned a surveying company, I use the language of that industry to explain what I mean.

If you look at love and relationships like landscapes, it's similar to how a surveyor maps out the terrain. We "mark" our territory or navigate through highs and lows, sometimes discovering a hidden gem. As you read about my life story, you will learn that not all relationships are equal and not all people mean well. Some are sublime and others are snakes.

At the end each chapter, you will find a STAKE IT! which refers to the stakes we use in the surveying world. Each stake is an anchor that I wish I knew about while going through the aftermath of losing My Robby. I strongly encourage you to take these stakes seriously and to find ways to "mark" your own territory with each. Because when you find yourself in a situation like mine, not only do the caring people show themselves. So do the coyotes and vultures.

LEFT: Me, the author. RIGHT: Robby catching a largemouth bass from our pond during my youngest son's going-away party to send him off to USMC Parris Island

CHAPTER 1
My Nightmare Begins

September 18, 2017, would begin the worst nightmare I have ever had. I was sitting in my car, alone, scared, and waiting for a callback. It was 4:15 a.m. when I received his last and final text, which I never expected to receive in this lifetime: not from My Robby. I never thought Robby would ever be able to cut me and hurt me so deeply that it would break my heart like it did. I thought our love would outlast any hurt the world could hurl at us.

The phone rang, and Alan asked me if I was alone.

"Yes, what's going on, Alan?"

"Can you pull over," he asked.

"Alan, just tell me what's happening."

"Tammie, just pull over."

***

It was 4:15 am, and I was getting ready to hit the road from a weekend at one of my best friends' houses in the Nashville area. I usually got on the road around 4:00 am to arrive back safe and sound at our home by 10:00 am, depending on how often my bladder didn't want to cooperate this trip.

I was up and hitting the shower by 4:05 and not really in a rush, so I took my time to ensure I was awake for the long trip back home alone. I sent Robby a good morning text and said I would see him soon, not so much expecting him to respond as hoping he would since he was usually up at 4:00 am getting ready for his day.

When I finished my shower, I realized I hadn't heard his ringtone go off yet, so I continued my process. At 4:18, his ringtone went off. My heart jumped, as always, but his response was strange this time. His response just hit me wrong.

It sent me back to Saturday afternoon when I told Shelley I felt something was wrong. My gut was usually right. However, Shelley told me it was probably because Robby and I had been arguing a lot lately, and he needed time to process whatever he was going through. So, I brushed off the feeling that I needed to head home early.

But his text was concise and to the point, not at all like him.

I am sorry that I am not the one who can protect you, Robby.

That was it. There was no, Love ya. Can't wait to see you, or Don't ever go away without me again.

What does that mean? I responded.

Within minutes, Robby still hadn't responded to me. And he still hadn't answered when I got on the highway. So, I sent another text asking him to stop playing games with me, saying that he knew I had a long trip ahead and that driving alone and not understanding what he meant made me very nervous and anxious.

I called his office at 7:00 am, but no one could find him. Monica said she had called and texted him several times without a response and that she, too, was getting anxious because it wasn't generally like Robby not to answer his phone after some tried to contact him several times. He was always very prompt, arriving at the office long before the staff did and ensuring that the field crews and drafting team were organized for their day.

I told Monica I would call one of my employees

to run to the house and check on him since my office was just one hundred yards away. I called John's cell, explained the situation, and asked him if he could make sure Robby was okay.

"Sure, Tammie. I'll call you back shortly."

By the time I got a callback, I had already made it to I-80. Traffic on the interstate on a Monday morning was very light then. But the next time I got a call, it wasn't John's voice. It was Alan's. Alan usually was very calm and polite, but today, he was firm and abrupt.

"Alan, just tell me what's happening," I pleaded.

"Tammie, just pull over."

But I kept driving and asking where Robby was. Alan got increasingly agitated and almost rude with his answers, to the point of giving me orders. I was in no mood for orders. Not when people weren't telling me where my husband and my whole world were.

"Tammie, pull the car over NOW!"

I pulled over and stopped the car. As he spoke, a whole lifetime of rage welled up inside me—feelings of betrayal. Feelings of being lied to. Feelings of abandonment by everyone who loved me or had ever claimed to love me. Why am I not enough? What did I do? I was unaware

My Nightmare Begins

at the time that suicide has nothing to do with those who are left behind. It's entirely about the one who left.

"Tammie?" It was Alan.

"I'm listening."

"Tammie, Robby is dead. He shot himself."

Silence.

"Wait, what did you just say? No, not my Robby! He promised me he would never do this. Not Robby!"

"Tammie? Where are you? Are you in a safe place?"

Time froze. I froze. I wasn't sure how to respond. The anger welling up in me took over. Then, the tears started, and bouts of sobbing overtook me, fits of anger and blind rage.

How could you do such a thing—to me, of all people? The one you swore you would never intentionally hurt, like every other man has in my life?

"Tammie, can Shelley drive you home, or do you need someone to get you?"

Home? Home is six-and-a-half hours away. But where is home if Robby isn't there? Robby built our house with his own hands. How can I be there without him now? How can it still be here standing without him?

I didn't even know where I was to have anyone pick me up, but I somehow found the ability to call Shelley. When she didn't answer, I called her husband, Paul. I tried to speak as calmly as possible so he could understand me. When what I said registered with him, he took over.

"Just sit there. I will find her and have her call you for a location."

Within two minutes, Shelley called me, asking for my location. She had to walk me through figuring that out. I saw a billboard that advertised a Shell gas station at Exit 4. She told me to go to that gas station, and she would be there as soon as Paul got home to drive her to me.

"And, Tammie? Don't get out of the car, lock the doors, and don't open them for anyone."

As I sat waiting, I called my cousin Troy, who was the county sheriff back home. He didn't pick up, so I left a voice message explaining what I had been told and that I was coming home. I asked him to take care of My Robby until I could get home.

I started calling our kids and remembered Robby's mom would soon see police and lots of cars at our house. So, I called a cousin she knew and asked if he could sit with her until one of her grandkids could get there.

My Nightmare Begins

Then I called my dad and my Nan. The last person I called was my cousin and best friend, Jarod. When I called Jarod, he hung up and called me back on FaceTime to see if I was safe. He always knew how to calm me and read my eyes when my voice might tell another story.

Within half an hour, Paul and Shelley arrived. A local sheriff's car appeared somewhere amid all of this. Later, I found out that my cousin had called the sheriff for that area and explained the situation, and they had a car sit and watch over me until Shelley got to me. As the sheriff watched us exchange tears and transfer Shelley's luggage to my car, I could see that was all he was there to do. And when we left, he went on his way. I was safe at last. My guardian angel, Shelley, had me, and we were on our way to face the nightmare. She would deliver me there safely.

This was the longest six-and-a-half-hour drive in my life. Calls started pouring in from concerned friends and family, and about three hours away from home, I got a call from Robby's new business partner, Mike. He informed me that he had spoken to the state of Mississippi and that I was now responsible for the balance of three hundred and sixty thousand dollars left on the promissory note my husband had signed just six months prior. I listened to his words and then, very briefly and to the point, asked him if he thought I was an idiot.

Of course, I added a few explicit words, informing him that he must have thought I was an uneducated country girl who didn't know my rights or the law and that I did not care what he or the state was trying to pull but my name was not on the promissory note that Robby signed. He could take that balance and shove it!

The snake I had seen just six months before, suspiciously signing his name faster than anyone I had ever witnessed before or since, finally showed his ugly, selfish, arrogant face as the person I had always known him to be. And I had just had my fill of him. After the confrontation, I called Fred, my attorney, and he assured me I was correct in what I had told him. Fred said the sweetest thing to me as we were about to hang up.

"I am so sorry. Robby was loved by many."

When Shelley and I arrived home around 3 p.m., I went to see Robby's mom first. Thankfully, I did because Robby's first wife pulled me aside and told me that some family members were trying to take some things from his mom's home. So, I had to put out those fires before getting to the crowd of concerned people at my own home.

My Nightmare Begins

Arriving at my home shortly after Robby's mom, I was almost bombarded by people I hadn't spoken to much since childhood. I finally got to the ones who protected Robby and our home from people who wanted to get in to see what had happened.

Derek, my cousin, whom I had called first before anyone else because I knew if he wasn't on duty at the fire station, he could get to Robby the quickest and protect him from onlookers and people who would try and take advantage of us. Derek's wife Michelle was there, too, along with my childhood best friend, Dana. I learned later that when Michelle went to Dana's classroom to inform her of the event, Dana bolted out of her room without telling anyone. In fact, she had almost gotten fired until someone explained to her what had happened and who I was. My dad, Nan, John, his wife Selma, and Allan were there, too. They were all the ones I needed to be near me more than anyone else until my boys arrived. My two sons and daughter-in-law had not made it in from Texas yet, and by this point, I was exhausted and emotionally dead.

My cousin Sandy had called my primary doctor of more than ten years, explained what had happened, and asked him to send in a prescription for Xanax so that I could cope with all the events of the day. And as my boys arrived, they came and found me and loved me through some harsh tears just as the Xanax was taking effect.

By 9:00 pm, I had a bedroom full of some of the most amazing women surrounding me, laughing, crying, and laughing again to the point that my dad thought I was having a nervous breakdown. I was coping, just not the way that he had, and he didn't know how he felt about the whole day.

Monday turned to Tuesday, then to Friday, and every day, I woke up more exhausted and confused than the day before. Tuesday morning, I started grief therapy called EET, and as I arrived home, I got a call from my husband's family attorney informing me that he had a visitor that morning. It would seem that Robby's ex-wife and two daughters thought that I had millions lining my bank accounts the second he died, and she wanted them to have their share. He hadn't been gone more than twenty-eight hours, and they were already trying to get their share. This was just the beginning.

The greed started the day after Robby's memorial when I invited his girls over to go through his things and pick out what meant the most to them. Instead, they emptied his closet, taking even his nasty yard sneakers, leaving me nothing.

"Okay, are we going to his office now?" they asked as soon as they were done.

"No. This is all I can handle today," was all I could say. I don't remember any tears other than mine that day. But their tears? They were laughing like it was Christmas Day.

I had payroll to take care of, two businesses with decisions to make, and one very hateful and greedy business partner who needed to be dealt with. I also attended several legal meetings to protect myself from Robby's partner, Mike. As I made the last business decision for his business, my attorney explained to me that I was not responsible for anything and that I should let him deal with the snake.

Fred, my attorney, called Mike and informed him that he was not to call me anymore. By this time, Mike had been calling multiple times a day, telling me to honor Robby's reputation by "doing the right thing" and paying his debt. I told him I would have no further responsibilities besides that week's payroll to his company. He ended up blocking me from the bank account. But before he could, I took out ten grand, even though Robby's company owed mine more than forty thousand by this point.

On Saturday at 10:00 am, more than three hundred heartbroken people came to pay their respects to my husband and to tell me that they loved me and would be praying for me and our family. That same night, my oldest son, ex-sister-in-law, and her husband left for Texas. The next day, my youngest son and his family left, heading back to Texas and offering to let me take their dog Lilly to keep me company for a little while until the shock wore off. I declined their offer, as I knew how very close my oldest grandson Wyatt was to Lilly. I didn't want him to have separation anxiety from her not being in his room at night if he woke up looking for her.

-------------STAKE IT!-------------

QUESTION: *On a scale of 1 to 5, how would you rank communication with your partner?*

CONSIDERATION: In committed, romantic relationships, communication is the foundation on which anything you both have is built. Like the cornerstone of a sturdy structure, effective communication establishes a clear channel for expressing your emotions, needs, and desires to your partner. When this communication is non-existent or undergoes a serious shift, the risk of negative outcomes escalates.

My Nightmare Begins

As surveyors who constantly examined the topography of the ground to avoid potential hazards, Robby and I had to keep the communication lines opened in our relationship, too. We did a great job for a while until stress in our marriage led to misunderstandings, resentment, and the erosion of trust and connection.

Challenge: Have you and your partner each share what the number one recent situation in your relationship could do with better communication. That's all for now, because knowing is the first step.

LEFT: Robby and me. RIGHT: Me and my sons, Jim (left) and Ronnie (right). Robby and I had taken separate pictures with our children on our wedding day. I no longer have the photo of him and his daughters because I was so angry after his death that I burned every photo of him within my reach.

CHAPTER 2

Getting to Know Us

Let me go back for a moment to show you what my first love looked like. He was short, but then again, we were only ten. He had mesmerizing blue eyes with a tiny scar under the right one that captured my heart from the beginning. His name was Robby, and his curls would make even the most obnoxious ten-year-old girl swoon. His crooked grin that lit up the world—well, mine—could make you smile, even when your world was at its darkest.

Robby and I were seventh-grade sweethearts, though it took him twenty-two years to profess that undying love in front of our children (from other marriages) and our small-knit community of family, friends, and parents of friends who helped raise us all.

In the beginning, it was like a bedtime fairytale from a book you would read to your child. Robby loved Disney World more than life all year. During winter, it was the Oakland Raiders (no matter who they were opposing). We visited Disney several times a year. He even took over the honeymoon planning and told me we were going to the Caribbean. But that actually turned out to be the Walt Disney World Caribbean Beach Resort in Florida. It was the only place where he would relax. Just seeing the Disney castle outside the airplane window would soften his exterior, and I would see that young, sweet, little, stress-free boy I fell in love with.

Then life took over. Months after reconnecting, we started our land surveying business on his fortieth birthday. We were committed to each other then and to our blended family of six. I gave Robby the boys he had always wanted, and he gave me my girls. The only problem was that ex-spouses and their problems came along with the blending of broken hearts.

In the middle of it all came more life, stress, and heartaches caused by each other and others from the outside. But what family doesn't endure those? Even the nonblended families have the same problems, I'm sure.

We took one day at a time, and we prayed that

we would not become another divorce statistic. We worked hard to overcome all the obstacles and believed true love would prevail. We prayed that we would be together for a long time: old, gray, and rocking in rocking chairs on the front porch with great-grandchildren all around us, eagerly waiting for Pappy or Nana to tell another funny story about their parents.

We were eager to learn everything we could about each other and even more: how to make each other smile when they wanted to cry their heart out and lean on each other when the world attacked you. We learned to see what the other needed before they asked, and we learned to say "I'm sorry" and how to mean it from the bottom of our hearts, even if we weren't in the wrong—to stop that brick wall from being built, or, perhaps, to show the other that they were being heard and that their feelings mattered.

On April 21, 2006, I arrived home from a weekend Easter trip to my parent's home to find an unexpected email on my online classmates. com account. At first glance, it was from someone telling me how sorry he was for being a horrible boyfriend when we were in high school. He signed his name "Robert."

I didn't remember dating anyone named Robert. I had only dated one guy in high school after moving back from Texas, and his name was Alan (we had been together for nearly two years). So I was confused, thinking that it might have been a mistake. The person didn't leave a phone number, so I couldn't call him to learn his identity.

After work, I logged into my account to see a new message, a phone number, and a different name—Robby. Suddenly, all of the jigsaw pieces fell into place, and all the years since the first time I had met Robby at ten years old—the mistakes I experienced, the poor choices I had made, and the long-lost thoughts about what our lives could have been suddenly—flooded my thoughts.

When you've had a spark with someone like Robby and I had, time stands still. No matter how long ago it was from the last time you saw or spoke to each other, it's as if there were no time lapses. So, I responded, emailing him my phone number.

It was as if he had been waiting for those ten little numbers to appear on his screen because my phone rang almost instantly. Robby's voice stayed the same. Sure, he was older, but that familiar sound stopped my heart like it did when we were kids.

We talked until 4:00 a.m. the following day about nothing and everything, wondering aloud why it had taken so long to reconnect and why we never got together in high school. He told me his heart stopped the first day I walked into Coach Thrash's drafting class. He had not seen me since the summer. When I sat right next to Alan, I was so close that he could smell my perfume and see the long, dark curls he had fallen in love with as a fourth grader. His whole world came crashing down around him. We talked like this every day for a week. The only time we weren't talking was at work, in the shower, or couldn't speak for whatever reason. Even then, we texted—finally, the tension of being apart built to the point that we could no longer handle it. We had to meet.

On April 29, we drove three hours to Lafayette from our respective cities. On that trip, I was at the end of a horrific rainstorm, and he was at the other end, going through it. It reminded me of the movie An Affair to Remember.

I arrived first, checked into the hotel, and waited for an eternity, praying that he would arrive safely. After nervously pacing, I resorted to a single-serve bottle of cheap wine from the hotel gift shop and took up a lookout post next to a lobby window, which gave me a clear view of the parking lot. I wanted to ensure I saw my lost loved one before he spotted me.

When a truck, matching the description Robby gave me of his own, backed into a parking space, I hid behind the curtains so he couldn't see me. It might have seemed childish of me, but I felt ten again. Concealed, I watched Robby walk up to the counter and ask that my room be transferred to his credit card. As I remained hidden, I quietly watched his every move to see if I could spot the one feature that would prove to me that he was Robby. And I saw it—that little scar under his eye. It was Robby.

At that moment, there was no need for me to hide. As I walked toward him, Robby turned to me, and we locked eyes. It was him, and that scar was my proof. As we reached each other in front of the lobby desk, he wrapped me in his arms and kissed me. You could have heard a pin drop (other than my crying) as the desk clerks reverently watched our reunion unfold.

"That's what true love looks like," one of the desk clerks told the other.

We all laughed out of nerves and joy, and then Robby and I disappeared into our room.

What do you do when you haven't seen your first love in decades? For us, we talked all night. Aside from affectionate hugs and kisses, Robby, like the perfect gentleman, never once tried anything out of line. He pulled out a red velvet box when we first got to the room.

"It isn't your necklace. Mom and I searched her house up and down and never found it, so I pray that this will replace it." When I opened the box, it was a gorgeous heart necklace with rows of round diamonds. And down one side, it was covered in baguette diamonds. He said he had searched every store in Gulfport and Biloxi before he found it. It was so perfect that I wore it with my wedding dress six months later. We finally fell asleep around 4:00 a.m. out of sheer exhaustion. Just as the sun peeked through the drapes, Robby rolled over, kissed me, and told me he would get breakfast while I showered.

Once I was done, we ate breakfast, talking around the muffins in our mouths and sips of coffee. Venturing from the hotel to spend time together, we discovered the International Festival and walked among the vendor booths. At one point, we stopped to share a hamburger and fries, sitting side by side in a booth as if we had been together for years. It was always supposed to be like this. I had never experienced this safe, calm feeling as quickly as this around anyone. We were trying our best not to look at our watches. But the day went by quickly, and we reluctantly had to return to the hotel to check out and go our separate ways.

As we packed our bags, we both cried, unashamed of the other seeing our tears and quietly wondering if we would ever see each other again. When you experience a reunion like that, paranoia or not, you don't want the other leaving your sight. Twenty-two years was a long time not hearing each other's voices and having all those old feelings come rushing back over one weekend.

Even when we left in our cars, Robby followed me for over twenty miles back to I-10. I was crying so hard that I finally couldn't stand it anymore. I pulled over on the side of the road and got out. Robby pulled in behind me and got out of his truck. I ran to him, crying so hard that he wouldn't let me get back into the car and leave until I stopped and had some control over myself. I finally composed myself while he reassured me that we would be together soon. We just needed to ensure that this (us) was truly what we each wanted.

Once we returned to the road, we talked on the phone for the entire three-hour trip. Once we each got back home, we continued to talk. It was like some force just wouldn't let us hang up!

On Monday, May 1st, I quit my job, picked up boxes, packed everything important to me, and drove to storage to put away what I didn't need.

I had spoken to my sons, who gave me their blessing, and they gave their blessing to Robby, too. The following Monday—fourteen days after the first email—I moved back to our tiny hometown of Lizana, Mississippi, the one place where I never wanted to live again. That wasn't because of the people of Lizana or because I had a bad childhood. Lizana was just too small, and everyone made it their business to know your business—sometimes even before you knew!

But this was Robby, the young boy who stole my heart decades ago. All those old feelings were back and stronger than anything I had ever felt on the romance scale. So, of course, I was willing to be back and finally have my "happily forever."

On May 8, I was supposed to leave at sun-up. I couldn't sleep and was up and out by 2:30 am. The whole way back to Mississippi, my heart raced almost as fast as I was driving. At one point, a Louisiana State Trooper was driving beside me. He rolled his window down and motioned for me to slow down. I think he saw how happy I was, singing and focused on the road, and how there wasn't anyone around me to injure except him. When I looked at my speedometer, I was doing 90 miles an hour. Somewhere along the way, I had put the car on cruise control. I guess that just wasn't fast enough for me.

***

Seeing Robby lying on the ice-cold slab in the funeral home and saying our final goodbyes was something no one should have to do. Robby had sustained such a drastic injury that we had to protect his head bandage to keep the exit wound from being exposed. When we saw Robby at the funeral home, he was draped in a beautiful red quilt that covered his chest and legs.

My boys and Robby's girls were there, along with Robby's ex-wife, who didn't come inside until I asked her to join us. My ex-sister-in-law, B, sat outside with the grand babies until I told her to come to say goodbye. Robby's mom, brother, wife and kids joined us also. Ronnie spoke to the funeral director, explaining that I had not seen Robby since the previous Friday and needed to see him alone. The morgue allowed me all the time I needed to be alone with him before anyone else, and I thought I was going to have a heart attack. I desperately wanted to hear Robby's voice, see the scar below his eye, and watch his eyes light up when he saw me. But I got none of that. All I could do was focus on him lying lifeless, yet so peaceful. I needed him to return to me and make this entire nightmare go away, take back all the hurt of the last year, and start over. It was a redo that we both deserved. Wasn't it?

His girls, ex-wife, brother, and mom (among others) were also there. When we each were calm again, we held hands and encircled Robby, reciting "The Lord's Prayer" together and praying for Robby's protection and covering as the Lord, whom Robby loved so much, welcomed him home.

------------STAKE IT!------------

QUESTION: *On a scale of 1 to 5, certain are you that you and your partner share the most important values?*

CONSIDERATION: Venturing into unknown territory when it comes to a romantic relationship should be approached with the precision and "knowing" of a seasoned surveyor. You can't just rush headlong into it and expect it to work out, so you need to distinguish between calculated and uncalculated risks. Calculated risks means evaluating things like compatibility, shared values, and long-term goals. Uncalculated risks happen when these considerations are overlooked or disregarded, like navigating blindly without a compass.

CHALLENGE: Have you and your partner each name the top three values you have in common that are as true today as they were when you met.

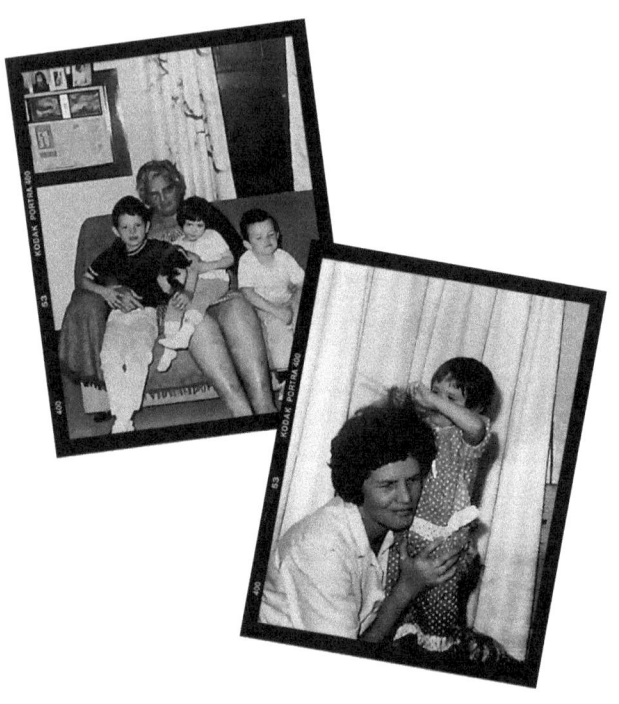

LEFT: My Granny Etha Mae (dad's mother) with us kids Michael (left), Danny (right), and me, and our dog Smokey. RIGHT: Me cutting my grandmother Clarice Odom's hair.

CHAPTER 3

Two Losses

1972 started as a great year. It was my first grade school year, and my Granny Etha, my dad's mom, walked me to my classroom, holding my hand and guiding me as she always had. She always knew just the proper amount of hand squeezing that I needed. That day, she was squeezing so hard that it almost cut off my blood flow. But it was well-intentioned, full of love, and very much needed.

The year quickly passed, and we were well into the summer vacation when a phone call came in. Getting off the phone, my Aunt Sandy told my Nan that my Maw Maw had passed and that she thought we needed to go and say our goodbyes. Maw Maw had driven to our house the Christmas before and brought us Christmas gifts. It was a big deal because it was a long drive for her. My mother's father was on the road again, so it was just her. But she had never done this before, and six months later, she was gone. We would never see her beautiful smiles, and I would never cut her hair again.

Maw Maw left her three girls and me with a unique trait. Her mother, her girls, me, and her second granddaughter Ashley (Aunt Sandy's daughter) all had the same tiny black mole under our right armpit. That was our special link to her. Every time I see mine, I think of her.

She had given me a hand-painted tin doll house with no details left out. The wooden shingles were painted on and looked so real that you could almost feel the wood grain. All the rugs in every room made your feet feel warm and comfy, just like at Grandma's house—right down to the curtains and furniture, including the baby's crib. She sat with me and played with me until it was dark. She told us she loved us, and I saw a tear in her eyes as she got in her car.

Our dad drove us over an hour away to the wake. He made his mom go with us, and Nan did, too. Dad dreaded seeing my mother. It had been years since he had last seen her, and he knew her husband, Len, would also be there. Dad walked me in, holding my hand and trying to keep out of sight, but it was useless. My mother was waiting at the

Two Losses

door for him—not us—him. She made a beeline for him, virtually ignoring us children.

It was sad and a very long night, but we all got through it. The next day would be another round as we watched Maw Maw being lowered into the ground. I had permanently bonded with her, unlike my brothers. Probably because I was her first granddaughter, and she loved letting me cut her hair with real scissors, too. She didn't care: she loved our time together, and I knew my little world would be less than perfect from that point on without her in my life.

In the coming months, school started again. And just like the previous year, Granny walked me where I needed to be. This time, it was to the bus stop, and she assured me that I would survive and do great.

Then, in October, she got sick and had to be hospitalized. A few weeks before, my Paw Paw had taken her to see someone in the hospital and had dropped her off at the door. He didn't realize that when she shut the door, her coat had gotten caught in the door, and he had dragged her around the parking lot, hitting her head. The ER checked her out and said that she had a concussion but would be okay.

She did have headaches and a giant goose egg that seemed to get worse over the next few weeks.

The hospital admitted her and found that a blood clot had formed. They gave her blood thinners to keep the clot from causing a stroke.

The night she passed, Nan had gotten a call in the middle of the night, letting her know that everyone needed to get to the hospital because she was not going to last much longer. She had already passed when they arrived. She had been hospitalized for over a month, and we never got to see her before she passed. She would always send "I love yous" with Nan for me with messages that she missed me and reminders of how much I loved to sing. That Christmas, when I opened the gifts she had gotten us kids before she got sick, I cried. She had bought me an organ of my own because she knew my love for music would only grow. I played that thing for hours every day.

I never got to say goodbye. I was only seven years old and had just lost both my grandmothers in the same year (not too many months apart). I could not imagine how our lives were going to be now. She was the rock that kept our family steadfast and the glue that held our family tight.

The following month was Thanksgiving, and Nan and I knew it would be hard, mainly on her, because Granny had always done all of the holiday cooking while Nan was at work. She and I had the task of figuring out how Granny made everything, from the pies, cakes, and candy to the cornbread dressing. It was exciting, but when the smells started coming to life, it didn't matter how good they tasted because we were crying one second and laughing so hard the next that we couldn't breathe.

Nan made Thanksgiving happen. As she cooked, I decorated our aluminum Christmas tree, installing the kaleidoscope wheel under it. As I watched the wheel light up, one of Granny's favorite Christmas songs came on, Kitty Wells's well-known song "C-H-R-I-S-T-M-A-S." I started crying almost to the point of gasping for air, and then Nan began to cry, too. Each year after that, it got a little better for us: her cooking became just as amazing as her momma's.

The next few years were a blur: nothing horrible, but nothing good. We were coasting through life like everyone else. Dad had remarried two years before his momma had passed and now had another daughter whom we saw a couple of times a month. We never saw his wife, Helen, not even on the holidays. I was already feeling pushed aside as a Daddy's girl who now had to share her time with him with another daughter. I was increasingly unhappy. For some reason, I found myself heartbroken all the time.

My second-grade year was rough. It seemed that

I was always sick after Granny passed. The following semester, after Christmas, I got sick and ended up in the hospital for over a month. I was scared to death. My older cousin Irma and her sister Janet would take turns staying with me because Nan had to work. One Saturday, Nan had left, and later, I heard my mother's voice. She appeared out of nowhere, telling me she was staying until I could go home and wasn't leaving me alone. After taking a nap, I asked my nurse where my mother was. All she said was that my mother had to go to work. I was abandoned again. Why did she even come? Did she enjoy torturing me? Why would she not just leave me alone?

My dad came every day on his lunch break and before he went home. I told him about my mother coming, and all he did was hold me while I cried (which made my throat hurt more, so they gave me another shot). By then, Irma was back for the night. Around this time, I learned how to resent someone: my mother. It was also the time I learned how to shut people out and build the proverbial brick wall. I got really good at this and learned that when I said I was done, there was nothing anyone could do to change my mind.

Fourth grade was a fantastic year for me. Without Granny to guide me, I was getting better at finding my way around, and Nan took over. She

Two Losses

always made me feel that I could do anything as long as I tried my best and put my mind to it and tried my best.

February was an exciting time. Every girl always awaited to see who would want to be her Valentine and who would get their hearts broken. This year was the beginning of rivals insofar as girls and boys were concerned. We were coming into our own, and I had a little girl who, since third grade, had it out for me. We just didn't hit it off anymore. We had formerly been best friends since we could remember, but something was off. I had met a new girl named Dana, and she and I were inseparable from the words "hello." This caused tremendous jealousy for the other friend, and she would not allow me to be happy outside of our friendship. She made that clear.

I was nominated for the fourth grade Valentine's Court, and each grade only got one. When my name was announced, the whole fourth grade gave a loud cheer. The look I got from that moment on was clear that my former friend was unhappy. I, on the other hand, was elated. I had never been nominated or awarded anything, much less a title like this. We had to wear formal gowns: my stepmother made mine. It was precious and made of a white cotton bodice and a red cotton skirt. The bodice had red hearts precisely placed, and the skirt had white hearts lining the ruffled edge. My Nan made me get an "updo"—she was always making me endure torture like that.

"I always wanted hair like yours, and it's beautiful," she would say. But no, it is insane and painful! My hair and head would hurt for days once all the pins came out.

It didn't take long before the new kid in our class noticed me, not her, and this started a new form of unhappiness for her. The day I met Robby, he could not stop smiling at me. And when he would smile, a tiny scar under his right eye would always perk up, and his piercing blue eyes would light up.

Robby was not the usual fourth-grade boy. He didn't tease or pull hair or make fun. He was shy, quiet, almost an introvert, and hard to read where feelings were concerned. Coming in mid-term, he was placed in Dana's class across the hall.

When we started fifth grade, we were all put into the same classroom and started changing classes a few times daily. He was seated in the chair next to me, and we both got caught not paying attention that year several times. As the year went on, he and I grew closer. Nothing started until seventh grade, but we knew there was something we had shared earlier.

He gave me a gift when we left for Christmas break in seventh grade. I opened it, and it was a crooked heart necklace with a tiny diamond chip on it. As we headed to the bus, he stopped me and kissed me under the two large oak trees. My head was spinning, and my heart was about to pound out of my chest! I couldn't breathe as he walked me, hand in hand, to my bus and told me to call him over the holidays.

But when we returned from break, he had broken up with me. I wondered what I had done in two weeks for him to change his mind. And that's when I saw him with my rival. He would break up with me every other day for her or her cousin. Indeed, she had it out for me because Dana and I were like inseparable twins. We still are today.

Dana and I have always been kindred spirits. Her parents accepted me as one of their daughters and Nan as hers. We each had chores at each other's houses and got scolded when we did something wrong. We both got caught smoking her mother's cigarettes when I almost burnt the barn down. She made us sit and smoke the whole pack. Dana got deathly ill, throwing up. Her mother responded, "I bet you won't ever do that again, will you? Then she called Nan.

We have a bond like only twins do. We both have similar health issues (like deafness in one ear, even though opposite ears). Our first weddings were a week apart and in different states. Our second sons were born days apart. As teenagers, we told everyone we were twins, just born to different parents. God felt sorry for one family dealing with both of us, so he split us up. Over the previous two decades, we had missed a couple of days talking to each other. When I moved back home, it was as if we hadn't skipped a beat.

When we returned for our eighth-grade year, I never accepted Robby's invitation for me to be his girlfriend. I told him I was done with his indecisiveness and that I didn't care anymore. So, I gave him back his necklace. That hurt me so much. I was already dealing with abandonment from my mother and some from my dad once my sister was born. But I could not deal with Robby doing it, too. I deserved better

We got through our last year of junior high, and he and I were still excellent friends. One Friday night at the skating rink, he walked up to me and kissed me. It was like we were back under the oak trees. I went home on Cloud Nine and loved him so much. It just never quit for us. No matter who or what came between us, it was us against the whole world. And no amount of time would change how we felt.

For our eighth-grade graduation trip, the entire class voted to visit the New Orleans French Quarter and Bourbon Street for the whole day. It was over an hour's drive in a school bus one way. On the way there, I sat with Dana, sharing our snacks and drinks, laughing, and telling jokes just like our class always did on every bus ride. We were all like family.

While there, Robby found me and asked if I would go on some rides with him, to which I agreed. When we rode the wooden roller coaster, I held onto him so tightly that I left fingerprints on his arms! When we were done riding the "tilt-o-world," he threw up. He could never handle twisting and turning rides—even the Tea Cup.

On the ride home, Robby asked Dana to swap seats with him so he could ride with me. I fell asleep on his shoulder, and we held hands the whole ride back.

-------------**STAKE IT!**-------------

QUESTION: *On a scale of 1 to 5, how much does the behavior of a former partner figure into your current one?*

CONSIDERATION: The behavior of a former partner can leave lasting imprints like scars on the landscape. By acknowledging past injuries and actively tending to emotional well-being, you can gradually restore trust in yourselves and others.

CHALLENGE: Have you and your partner share how *different* you both are than previous partners.

LEFT: Me. RIGHT: Robby. These are school photos from our 6th grade. If you look carefully, you can see the tiny scar under Robby's right eye that would help me identify him twenty-two years later.

CHAPTER 4

Young Love

My name is Tammie Elaine Osborne, and I was born a Lizana to Jerry, a Marine, and my mother, Betty, on January 5, 1966, in the most gorgeous place I have ever seen: Honolulu, Hawaii. My dad was stationed there as a young military police officer (MP) with the United States Marines to guard Pearl Harbor. My birth mother, Betty, didn't work outside of the home, and our family lived on base in military housing. Before they were blessed with my presence, as my dad says, they had three sons: Michael, born in Mississippi; Jason, born in North Carolina; and Danny, born in West Virginia. Each of us was born two years apart. My mother once told me that we were planned that way. But how could she have meant we were "planned" when she let us go so easily?

Though Honolulu was beautiful, it also brought heartache to my parents. My brother Jason, who was born with half of his stomach missing, passed away in 1964 while my parents were stationed there. My brother Danny was only six months old when Jason passed away, and he was first introduced to our extended family when my parents flew home to bury Jason, which also happened to be on my dad's sister's birthday, July Fourth. My parents stayed only as long as the Marine Corps would allow them for emergency leave. I made my entrance two years later.

I was born two months premature and (from what I've been told) came out fighting for my life, fighting for my place as the only girl in the family at the time, and fighting to run the family. That didn't quite work out as I expected, but I did order my brothers around for a little while before my orders fell on deaf ears. I was born with porcelain-white skin, mounds of dark curls, and large dark brown eyes. From what I can see in family photos of my infant years, I was already a daddy's girl by then. In all honesty, I still am.

On July 19, 1966, a family in San Leandro, California (close to San Jose) welcomed their fourth and youngest child, a little boy named after his dad's uncle. Named Robert Nathan Os-

Young Love

borne, they nicknamed him Robby. Robby was a very active boy. Growing up, his dad had been blacklisted in the machinist union, and his parents decided to move to be near his mom's family again in the little town of Long Beach, Mississippi, which was not too far from the coast. They owned a cute house in a quiet coastal town and attended good schools. Their school was close to the beach, which Robby's brother David loved. David had long blonde hair and a tan. All the girls loved him and thought he was "cool."

But when Robby was four, his family moved everything they could across the country to make a fresh start where no one knew his dad. Back then, there was no internet or social media to look up people as easily as it is today. The move wasn't necessarily because Robby's father had done anything legally wrong. He simply didn't agree with some of the "dirty" books that his wife was required to keep for his boss out West. It was easier to leave. But David wasn't happy about the move.

In 1967, my dad was called back to the mainland and given orders back to Camp Lejeune, where he would be processed to fight in the Vietnam War. We were at Camp Lejeune for a year before he left to go overseas. While he was gone, my birth mother, two brothers, and I ended up moving to Gulfport, Mississippi, to live with my dad's parents and sister Julia, whom I now call Mom. Sometime after this, my mother moved us to Lucedale, Mississippi, to be near her parents and sisters so they could help care for us—mainly because she didn't like my dad's mom.

While my dad was in Vietnam, our mother ended up leaving us with her parents and younger sister, Aunt Sandy. I later learned that she left us with her younger sister and ran off with a truck driver she met at her father's truck stop. She never returned except for a few holidays here and there. It always seemed like our little broken hearts were always on the mend from as early as I can remember. She met someone else and decided motherhood wasn't her cup of tea.

At twenty-one, when she had me, I was her fourth child, and she was just a child herself. My birth mother was just fourteen when Michael was born and bore three more children before the age of twenty-one. She didn't know how to be a mother because she was just a child who hadn't had the best childhood. I later learned that she and I shared one horror: her father sexually abused her and me. She never indicated whether or not her two sisters were subject to the same treatment, and I never asked.

When my dad came home from his deployment in Vietnam, his mother-in-law greeted him at the airport: no wife, no kids—just my Maw Maw. While she drove him home, she had to explain that his children were scattered all over the East Coast with my aunts and that she had not heard from our mother since she left. The one thing she didn't tell him was about my abuse because they knew that would have sent him into a blind rage. He might have even killed my mother's father had he known.

My Maw Maw drove my dad to his parents' home, which was over an hour away. Upon telling his parents everything that had happened, he borrowed his parents' car (my mother sold his 1965 Bel Air, which he had always wanted) and some money for gas and food because his pay had yet to be deposited. He was on a mission to find his kids.

He found Danny with Aunt Sandy in Mobile, Alabama. He saw Michael, who was with my birth mother's parents in Lucedale, Mississippi. He found me in West Virginia with Aunt Debbie and Uncle Tom.

When he arrived at Aunt Debbie's, she begged him to let her keep me. She promised him that she would give me the best of everything and that I would not go without anything. He refused because her father was a predator (my mother had told him about a few incidents in her childhood). He knew I would be around him more if I stayed, and that was more than he was comfortable with. He found all his kids and took us to his parent's house, where he knew we would be safe, surrounded by many aunts, uncles, and a slew of cousins within walking distance and as much love as we could handle and wanted. We kids were covered with love and laughter.

My dad's sister, Julia Charlene, raised me. I called her "Nan" or "NanNan" (now "Momma)." Unlike my birth mother, she never grew tired of us.

Growing up, we only lived with the bare necessities of life. We didn't have a traditional home life where a mom and dad raised their family together, teaching them all they needed to know to help them mature and contribute to society once they left the nest. For example, we didn't know what romance or falling in love looked like except to watch our friends' parents.

Nan never dated, and until last year, I never knew whether or not she had ever kissed anyone. She told my sister and me that she had kissed someone, and I believe it was special. She blushed when she told us, but she wouldn't give details. Her father was rigorous and old-fashioned. He thought that the last-born daughter should build her life around caring for the family's elders, which meant not being allowed to have a family of her own. She was so beautiful, with not a mark on her skin: perfect, like a China doll. Her hair was wavy, dark brown, and she always wore it short. She was sweet, quiet, and reserved yet very much attuned to the world. Her whole life was work, her dad, us kids, and church.

Nan and I shared a bedroom until I moved away the summer before my ninth-grade year of school. She had sat me down and told me that if I ever dreamed of having a husband and my own family one day, I would have to move out of my Paw Paw's house because he would never allow me to date. So, with my broken heart again, I reluctantly packed my belongings and moved to my dad's house, hoping that this time would be better than the last one.

I would spend at least a week or two of my grade school and junior high summers with my birth mother's younger sister, Aunt Sandy, babysitting her children while she and my Uncle Jerry would work. Today, Aunt Sandy and Uncle Jerry still hold a special place in my heart.

One summer, Aunt Sandy came to pick me up. When we got closer to her home, she asked if I wanted to visit my mother. I was a little apprehensive (this wasn't the only time she had asked me this question), and she could tell. When she asked me what was wrong, I couldn't find the words to answer her. All I knew was that something didn't feel right.

When I relented, Aunt Sandy told me that I needed to be aware that my birth mother had a "new baby," which ended up being a toy poodle named Pierre. He was a bundle of soft, coal-black, wavy fur—just precious—but I couldn't get Aunt Sandy's words "new baby" out of my head during that entire visit. If Pierre yelped, I got fussed at. There were many nights that I went to bed and cried myself to sleep because I could see that my birth mother loved that dog more than she loved me. How do you love an animal more than a child you created?

I didn't take my feelings out on Pierre because he was innocent. Though a child, I was smart enough to know that Pierre didn't abandon me at the age of two when my dad was ordered to Vietnam to fight for his life. It was my birth mother. I recall many more visits when she made promises she broke or just outright lied to me. I finally stopped wanting to see her, including not wanting her to send me birthday cards (usually weeks after my birthday). The only birthday she ever got right was my brother Michael's, her firstborn. Years later, on the day that her father died, she explained that Michael was the child who saved her from her horrible childhood.

In the seventh grade, my dad talked to Danny and me about moving in with him. I had already had my fill of life with a stepmother, and I already knew that if we did move in, my dad's life would not be good. His wife didn't want another woman's children in the house living with her—especially a daughter. She just couldn't deal with that. For that to happen would be like her acknowledging that he had been with another woman before her who had given him his first daughter. It would have felt like a betrayal. She pretty much confirmed that a few years later when I moved away to Texas to live with my birth mother for my sophomore year in high school.

In ninth grade, all my childhood friends got to ride the bus from Lizana, where we grew up together, just like we all did after ball games and field trips. I had to ride with strangers who looked down on me like a peasant girl with hand-me-down clothes because my stepmother never wanted to buy me new clothes like she did for my little sister. My dad had to beg her to take me shopping, and it constantly caused a family fight almost to the point of divorce.

One evening, my stepmother came home late

after my sister and I had to fend for ourselves for dinner. She walked through the doors and announced that she had gone shopping for us. We ran down the hall and into the kitchen only to see that my sister had gotten Polo shirts and Gloria Vanderbilt jeans (which were all the rage back then). And what did she get me? *Palmolive dish soap.*

I stood in the kitchen fighting back the tears, not wanting her to see how deeply hurt I was. Maybe she had overheard me telling a friend that I felt like I was Cinderella living with her: constantly dusting, cleaning, and doing laundry when my sister never had to do anything. It took me until I was forty years old before I could pick up a bottle of Palmolive again. And it was then that I needed to forgive her to move on and be healed.

The summer after ninth grade, I was playing in my first women's softball tournament at our little church's annual bazaar. I felt so grown up. You had to meet a specific age requirement and be invited to play to make the team. I was so proud of myself.

At about the halfway mark of my first game, I looked toward the fence line and saw my birth mother's father and his wife standing there, smiling and clapping as we took our turns to bat. I hugged them and told them I couldn't talk because I had to take my spot on deck to bat. They found places to sit and watch the game, and when it was over, they drove me to my Paw Paw's house, where they convinced me to leave the tournament early and drive to Texas with them.

When I called my dad to ask if I could spend the summer in Texas and return for my sophomore year of high school, he said yes, as always. But then he warned me to watch myself around my mother's dad. At fifteen, I had only noticed how my skin would crawl when I was around him. Surely, it couldn't be so bad now that he had a normal wife.

The second morning into the trip to Texas, we were in Hattiesburg visiting his sister when his wife and sister walked to a little store across the street. I was sitting on the couch watching TV. He walked over, sat next to me, put his hands in places where they didn't belong, and told me that I needed to stay sitting down because these were the things boys would want to do. His rationale was that I needed to get used to these things.

The very moment I jumped up, his wife and sister walked in. His wife realized something had happened and asked me if I was okay. I walked away, shaking and wanting my dad so desperately. But I knew that if I called and told him, he would kill the man who was supposed to be my grandfather, and I would lose my dad. So, I said nothing, and she left it alone until we got to Texas. I went straight to the room that would be mine for the summer and started crying. I was so nauseous and scared when she walked in and saw me.

I ended up telling her everything. She said that he had also done those things to her infant granddaughter.

"How can you still be with him?" I asked, horrified.

"I had nowhere else to go," was her response.

Then she "fessed up" and told me someone across the street wanted to see me.

"Who? I don't know anyone here?"

"Your mother."

"Oh, she's visiting?"

"No. She lives across the street."

"Well, I guess that was an unimportant detail you failed to share with me."

-------------**STAKE IT!**-------------

QUESTION: *On a scale of 1 to 5, how much do old relationships disrupt your ability to enjoy your current romantic relationship without resentment?*

Young Love

Consideration: You have and will encounter both easy and difficult obstacles. In navigating these with your romantic partner, resilience is like the sturdy equipment in the surveyor's kit. Similarly, flexibility with boundaries is a crucial adjustment mechanism in your toolbox for adapting to the changing landscapes you have and will encounter. Just as a skilled surveyor adjusts their approach to accommodate shifting ground, you must remain open to renegotiating boundaries in relationships to maintain harmony and balance.

Forgiveness of past injuries is key. It's like a surveyor repairing damaged equipment to ensure they make accurate measurements. By practicing resilience, flexibility, and forgiveness, you can navigate the complexities of romantic relationships with grace and precision.

Challenge: Consider how an old relationship with a parent, sibling, relative, boss, or romantic partner interferes with your current partnership. Could you do with more resilience, flexibility, or forgiveness?

LEFT: Me, in my cheerleading uniform. I used to cheer for Robby's football and basketball teams. RIGHT: Robby in his football uniform: the Lizana Wolverines. We're both in the 7th grade.

CHAPTER 5

It's Complicated

The ninth-grade year was horrible. I had just moved from my Paw Paw's house and knew no one on my bus route. I rarely saw my friends from Lizana anymore and had acne from hell on top of it. I was living with my dad and stepmother now and not very happy. Having had so much heartache and trauma in my short thirteen years, I wouldn't say that life was going that well.

I had tried to live with my stepmother for a short, two-day stint when I was in the seventh grade because my dad talked me into it. He checked me out of my old school on a Wednesday and enrolled me in a new school near their house on Thursday. By Friday, I told him I didn't want to stay there anymore.

On Thursday morning, I was enrolled in my new school, and my stepmother woke up my half-sister for school to get her ready (she was in second grade). While she was getting ready, I overheard my stepmother tell my sister that she did not intend to raise someone else's child. I waited until she left for work to tell my dad.

"She would never say that," he said.

But I know what my young ears heard. From then on, I decided I was not staying where I was not welcomed. That following Monday morning, I returned to my old school, where everyone knew me and could not wait for me to get there.

I saw Robby in the hallway one day, standing next to his new best friend, Kenny. Seeing him for the first time in a long time, he looked like he didn't know who I was. I had on an old ripped fake leather jacket and wanted to die. It was like he was looking everywhere around me except at me. I was so broken after that.

Whenever I saw Robby or his friend, I would dart down another hallway. I couldn't handle the shame and heartache anymore. I didn't want to see or hear from him again.

One day, I was walking into English class, and his friend Kenny was walking out. When I got to my desk, there was a note with my name on it.

Kenny had written me a love note, and all I could think was, *What in God's name is this?*

When I responded to him, a girl saw me give him the note, and the next thing I knew, I had a furious girlfriend on my hands. She didn't want to hear anything I had to say, so I showed her the note from him that started the whole thing, and needless to say, she and I became good friends. The rest of that year was smooth. Kenny continued to flirt, and I did not.

~Mommy Issues~

As I mentioned previously, I had an encounter with my biological mother's dad in which he sexually assaulted me in Hattiesburg at his sister's house when I was sitting on the couch in the livingroom watching television. Thank God that his wife walked in when she did, or the situation might have gotten worse.

Needless to say, I kept my distance from him on the six-hour road trip to Texas that next day, though he insisted I sit next to him. I left off the story after mentioning that his wife, aware that something was off, approached me in private and asked me if the he had put his hands on me. It was in that conversation that she also educated me on my new neighbors—mainly one in particular: *my birth mother.* She lived directly across the street. Go figure.

But then there was another neighbor whose name was Craig. Craig was a chiropractic student from Dallas who was so handsome that it took one's breath away. He had short blonde hair and sky-blue eyes. And as luck would have it, there wasn't a female in sight anywhere. I had an instant, undeniable crush on him but kept a respectful distance until my step-grandmother saw what was happening. Every moment after that, she would find reasons for me to go to his trailer. He started asking me questions, and I quickly filled him in, though I was shy about sharing.

When my birth mother found out I was at Craig's, it didn't take her long to kidnap me and build up my hopes that I would be moving to Texas.

I will not go back on the road. I will be a mother to you. It will be different. I promise.

Around this time, I met my stepsister Paulette for the first time. She was very sweet and pretty with long, beautiful, dark blonde hair. She wore thick glasses and was very naive to the world (not that I wasn't), but she was worse off than

I was—like she lived in a cave. When she was younger, her father, the man that my birth mother ran off with at the truck stop, had divorced his wife. Paulette's maternal grandfather was a wealthy man. He took the kids from his daughter and gave them to a state home in Decatur, Texas, where they lived until they turned eighteen. They were then turned out into this ugly world with nothing but their clothes and photos.

At the end of the summer, my birth mother told me to get dressed and that we both were going to downtown Houston. I had been to Houston several times, shopping with her and my stepsister, so I didn't think anything of it. I got dressed, and off we went. When we walked into a ten-story office building, I quickly realized I was there for her to take me away from my dad. She didn't ask me how I felt about this, and I don't think she cared either.

As we sat, they talked. They never asked me my opinion or concerns, only if I thought my dad would fight her on it, and I honestly told them that he never tried to keep her from us. She just never came around much, which got me into trouble later that day.

When she visited, we were always allowed to spend as much time with her as we wanted, so long as it didn't interfere with our school schedule. I always knew when she was coming because she would park her eighteen-wheeler truck at the corner store, two hundred yards from our house. I could always hear it. I could also hear her truck engine growing fainter in the distance when she left us. It was always hard for me when she left. I felt as if I was losing her for good, and feeling that kind of abandonment all over again each time she visited was more than I could bear.

That weekend, we had planned to drive back to Mississippi to pack up my things and move me to Texas. We arrived at the Dole Port in Gulfport, where I later learned she had regularly picked up bananas to haul wherever they needed to go. It was only a twenty-minute drive from where I lived, and she never called to check on us or ask to see us. When it came to her children, it was out of sight, out of mind.

When we returned from moving me to Texas, my mother was cooking dinner when she asked if I wanted cheese on my salad. When I told her I didn't know, she called me a selfish, spoiled bitch. How did not knowing that such an ingredient even went on a salad make me worthy of that title? Even my stepmother didn't call me that. We didn't have those sophisticated luxuries at my Paw Paw's house. Cheese was on hamburgers on "Hamburger Wednesdays," and it was in the mac and cheese that went along with it. She knew what our finances were. She had once lived there, too.

Later that night, my mother entered the room I shared with Paulette. She told me that she was staying home off the truck and would be a mom to me again. I heard my stepdad tell her later that he didn't sign up for raising kids and that they were a truck-driving team, which meant two drivers, not just one. He also told her she was not staying home, so she left me again a week later, without any care or concern for me being fifteen, with the only supervision being a sex-craved pervert of a grandfather who lived across the street. I felt abandoned, trapped, and terrified of that man she left to keep an eye on Paulette and me.

I have consistently felt this way about her since she learned that my half-sister's birthday was a day before mine. She would call me on her birthday to wish me a happy birthday. She managed to do this each year when I didn't have her number blocked. She would laugh about it when I called her out on it, which led me to block her for years—until something happened that made me unblock her.

The summer going into my junior year of high school, I told my mother I wanted to spend it with my best friend Dana, not knowing that I was never planning to return to Texas. She finally agreed, not realizing I wasn't asking permission. I was moving back to Mississippi, whether she approved it or not. She had lied to me, trying to get my dad to give her custody instead of the annulment that he had asked her for so that he and his wife could marry in the Catholic church. That was why she dragged me to the ten-story office building downtown the summer before.

Leaving the safety and love of NanNan's home by going to my dad's home and a new school created an environment that was less loving than the one I had left. I always felt like an outsider at my dad's house. I never felt like anyone acknowledged me unless the kitchen wasn't cleaned, the furniture wasn't dusted, or Dad's uniforms needed to be ironed. I knew it wouldn't be easy, but my time with them in the seventh grade showed me how hard it would be.

One day, I came home from school, and my stepmother sat my sister and me down at the kitchen table to announce that she and my dad were getting divorced.

"Your father and I have placed a bet on who wants to live with who."

This was my senior year, and I didn't have

much longer to deal with this. I would be off to college and start my own life, or so I thought. In the spring of 1984, just weeks before my graduation, I was asked to join my new boyfriend and his family on a going-away trip for him because he was joining the Air Force. My dad agreed, and we left to go to his soccer game. When he dropped me off to pack afterward, I found a note from my dad telling me he had talked to my stepmother and decided it was not a good idea. Well, I left them a note telling them I was moving out.

In May, I graduated. The night of my graduation, I never saw any of my family—not my dad or even NanNan. Though NanNan said they were there, my dad had gone fishing. I had a scholarship to American Beauty College, and all expenses were paid. But instead of doing that, I moved back to Texas.

~Rekindled~

Moving cross country from California to Mississippi was an adventure for Robby. He drove with his dad, and his brother David rode with his mom to help with the driving if she got tired. Robby and his dad were the lead vehicle, the moving van, and they drove much faster than

Robby's mother.

While en route to Las Vegas, Robby's mom, trailing behind the lead van by a long shot, got lost and somehow had to find Robby and his dad. There weren't cell phones or pagers back then, as it was in the early 1970s, so she couldn't just call to find out where they were. They had preplanned places along the way where they would gas up, so she headed to the next one on the map.

When she finally found them, Robby's dad had found a convenience store with scratch-off machines in the entrance. His dad let Robby buy a few to scratch off while waiting for his mother to recall which store they would fill up at. When she finally arrived and saw Robby "gambling," she reamed her husband out, though Robby had a great time doing it.

The next day was Robby's fourth birthday. He remembered stopping at the Grand Canyon, where his brother tried to push him off the side. Not only was David unhappy about having to move, but he was also unhappy with sharing the one parent who loved him more (his father) with Robby, which everyone says they knew was not true. David just made careless choices and needed a firmer hand to keep him in line than his mother gave him. Robby's mother constantly interfered with his dad's disciplining David to aggravate the situation. For example, she would tell him to stop getting onto David whenever he was home too late. This, as you can imagine, gave David mixed signals.

Torturing Robby seemed to be David's favorite pastime. As they grew up and older, David would always find ways to show how jealous he was of Robby, and when grown up with wives and children of their own, it was still an issue. In some respects, things got worse. Robby was always the one taking care of their mom, while David left her worrying almost daily.

One night, their mom came home crying because she was sure she had seen David on a corner she had passed by while leaving work. She said she had seen a man on the street asking for food and money. She was sure it was him and claimed that when he saw her, he turned away so she would not see his face.

Mother's Day weekend of 2011 was just like all others. Robby's mom always wondered where David was and hoped to see him one last time before she passed. It was such a hard way to live, not knowing where your child was and not knowing whether or not he needed anything, if he was hurt, if he was hungry, or if he was warm. But that year would be the last time that she had to worry about David.

I was in Dallas for a women's Christian weekend with one of my best friends and now ex-sister-in-law, Barbara. My boys and I have always called her B., and B and I had married brothers. Even when we divorced the brothers, we kept in touch with each other and their mother, Kathryn. Kathryn was a blessing to us both. At one time or another, while married to her sons, we had both lived with her.

Kathryn had taught me to cook and sew. She was a seamstress, making the most fabulous clothes and bedding, even designing curtains and bedding for a builder's model home. She created gorgeous wedding dresses that would make every bride's dream come true: dresses covered in lace and beads with long trains to match. She was always so busy doing that. But once people got her number, she had to turn people away.

While driving back to Houston that Saturday from the women's weekend, I got a phone call from Robby, telling me that David had been hit by a drunk driver while driving to the store. David had been sober from drugs for nearly ninety days at the time, and Robby and I had decided to help finance rehab for him. David had a daughter, and her world revolved around her daddy. All he wanted was to be a good dad to her and her half-sister, a girlfriend's daughter.

Somebody told us that he had been driving to the store, and an oncoming truck hit him square in the front of his truck. It was so bad that when the drunk driver went to court, the judge told him that he could not have squared up his vehicle better had he tried. David's head hit the roof so hard that it caused a blood clot, leaving him fighting for his life, and the doctors could not operate on him until the next day due to the amount of swelling in his brain.

Like in previous years, I had gotten up at 3:00 a.m. to drive six hours home, going straight to Memorial Hospital, where David was. David had not yet been taken to surgery, so we all saw him one last time. He was conscious enough to tell his Momma "Happy Easter" instead of "Happy Mother's Day." He quietly whispered to me as I bent over to kiss his cheek.

"Please take care of my momma for me." Then he spoke to Robby.

"I will see you soon, little brother." That was the last and sweetest thing he had ever told Robby.

There were tears in Robby's eyes when I turned to watch them wheel David's bed into the operating hall. I could only hug him tightly as we walked his mom into the waiting room. I stayed with the family until Robby's sister and husband arrived. When I knew they would be okay, I left to go home and rest a little bit. Two hours later, I received a call that David was doing well, and the doctors told the family they could all go home.

At 10:45 p.m., I received another phone call from the hospital. David's blood pressure was unstable, and he had started slipping away. We needed to come to the hospital. As we all got up and dressed, the hospital called back to tell us that David had passed. We called his sons, sister, and brother in California, and everyone met at the hospital. It was one of my saddest memories, being in the car on the way to the hospital because Robby kept talking about how Osborne men never lived beyond age 50.

No matter how often I had proven to Robby that his father had lived to see 50 ½ years (and now David at 52), he could not understand that he had broken the so-called Osborne curse. Robby's resistance to my logic felt as if he were making it so that it became real. I could not wrap my head around it. This was the beginning of the end for us. Our love for each other should have been enough to pull him out of this. He started finding fault with everything I did and said—even telling me to wear tight jeans and shirts to a client's office to get more work. When I refused, it made him more upset.

That situation in the car took me back to before Robby had found me again. It was Easter weekend, April 2006. I had driven home for the holiday, which was always my favorite. "New beginnings" is how my boys and I always saw it. I had stayed at my dad's house in Diamondhead, and my cousin and his wife came to see me. They were talking about their mare giving birth to the most gorgeous foal they had ever helped birth. Being who I am, I went to see it for myself.

So, I had driven my niece and nephew to see what the foal looked like. As I talked to my cousin's wife on the farm, I noticed Robby's mom's house was across the field from theirs. I asked her if she had seen Robby lately, and she pointed across the pond to Robby's mother's house: a large ranch-style home with a large front porch and a bay window by the kitchen.

I recalled a conversation Robby and I had in his drafting class one morning when I sat beside him, waiting for my boyfriend to get to class. Robby asked me what my favorite style of house was. I had told him that the style of house I preferred was one with a large porch where I could grow old with my husband, sitting in matching rocking chairs as our grandkids ran around, fill-ing the air with laughter. At the same time, we watched sunsets and celebrated the holidays with our family and kids.

In drafting class, he was assigned to create a style of home, draw it, and submit it for grades. Little did the students know that their drawings were also being judged for competition and that the winner would represent their class at the state competition that year. I had dreamed of having the house that Robby drafted one day, not realizing it would be with him.

The house that Robby eventually built from those plans was perfect. It had white tile floors, solid doors, and a large kitchen with many cabinets, which he had built with one of my cousins, who we later learned was his mom's nephew. He hand-built every piece of trim and molding, ran the plumbing, and installed every fixture perfectly. The only things he had to hire out were the electrical and the backhoe to build the foundation.

As a surveyor, to have your home perfectly sitting due north means that in winter, the corner of the home will block the north winds, and in summer, the garden will also be protected. It also means that the front of the house faces due south. And in feng shui, prosperity, happiness, and love will flow through your home so long as nothing inside blocks the blessings. Robby built his home with that in mind. When he found me, he told me that his drafting assignment was based on the design I told him I liked, and he had taken it to the state competition, where he placed second overall in the whole state of Mississippi. Robby and his family lived in this home for five years. In May of 2006, it was finally mine.

When I was at the farm to see the foal and looking across the pond at Robby's house, my heart was heavy for Robby, and I couldn't figure out what it was. After all, I had not heard from him for more than twenty years. On May 28, 1984, at our high school graduation, Robby hugged me when we were disbanding and told me he would miss me. But he never told me how he felt about me. That would have changed everything and spared both our sets of kids' lives of heartache and fear. It also would have spared me from emotional and physical abuse.

When I got home from the Easter weekend visiting my parents and meeting my cousin's foal, the whole drive home, I felt like I was trying to bring back to life an old me: the little ten-year-old who first met Robby. It had been surreal to be across the field from his home, seeing how he kept it up and how much love and care he had put into it, even from a distance.

As I mentioned, on Monday, April 21, an email from classmates.com awaited me, and we met each other shortly after. When we had to leave each other, and I ended up pulling over on the side of the road, we got out of our cars, and he held me while I sobbed.

"What's wrong?" Robby asked while cars zoomed by us at Exit 103-A, Evangeline Thruway, Lafayette, Louisiana.

"I don't want this to end," was all I could say.

"Me neither."

From that point on, he asked me to decide what I wanted. Later that week, I drove to Mississippi on a Wednesday to see my parents. Robby had asked if my son had found a car yet. As I told him no, he offered his old truck to my son. Shocked, I told him I could pay for it.

"You and I are starting a great relationship. Your sons are my sons now. Bring your son, Jim, with you so he can drive it back."

That was the proposal. And I accepted.

------------**STAKE IT!**------------

QUESTION: *On a scale of 1 to 5, how much of your self-worth, needs, and concerns do you feel are allowed to be expressed in your current relationship?*

Consideration: Navigating the dynamics of old and new family relationships is like encountering different landscapes marked by varying degrees of familiarity on one hand and difference on the other.. Much like a seasoned surveyor who carefully charts courses across complicated ground, you need to skillfully navigate old and new family bonds, balancing the comfort of the old ones with the excitement of the new.

Establishing your own self-worth is like staking a sturdy anchor or having a steady landmark guiding your way through shifting landscapes. By recognizing and affirming your value, you can build healthy, fulfilling relationships, free from the distortions of past wounds.

Furthermore, seeking independence within a new romantic relationship is like the surveyor's quest for autonomy, allowing you to maintain a sense of power and self-direction while navigating the shared journey of partnership. By being independent, you can still collaborate with others while maintaining your own individuality.

Challenge: Have you and your partner each share one thing that has been on your mind lately. The other partner doesn't need to do anything but listen for now.

ABOVE: Robby and me on a Christmas
Cruise in 2015 and still very much in love
BELOW: Robby and I n San Antonio, Texas, on
family vacation. We had been at a fiesta all day
and then went to Red Robin Restaurant to eat
amazing burgers for dinner. His tiny scar
is showing in both photos.

CHAPTER 6

Blending Our Lives

When Robby met Jim, I was afraid it would be awkward for them. But oddly enough, it was as if they had always been a part of each other's lives. I met Robby's oldest daughter, Jade, who didn't seem to care much about meeting us. Later, we learned that the truck Robby gave Jim was supposed to be Jade's when she turned sixteen. So, strike one already.

Later that evening, Robby took me to dinner with him and his girls. Katelynn was great, but Jade, understandably (because of the car incident), kept staring at me like I was the "step monster" with a wart on her nose. It was a great dinner, where the server sat us next to the fireplace. In April, you would have thought this steakhouse wouldn't have the fireplace burning, but it added to the ambiance: lots of families, quiet music, and great food. Also, the company was like a dream, plus two kids who seemed only to want to get to know me if I could give them what they wanted.

Robby joined me every day at my dad's house and even followed me there the at 5:00 the morning that Jim and I left to drive back home. My dad had pulled Robby aside and asked him what his intentions were with me.

"Sir, I have loved her my whole life, and that will not change. I pray she loves me back for the rest of my life." My dad smiled and shook his hand.

It was noon when Jim and I arrived back in Houston, and Robby and I had been talking a lot. He was busy dealing with the aftermath of Hurricane Katrina and the devastation along the Mississippi Gulf Coast. Everyone thinks that Katrina hit New Orleans, but the truth is that it hit Pass Christian, Mississippi. Hurricane Katrina claimed thousands of lives. Homes slid off their foundations and could be found next door on their neighbors' property. Some houses were never found—with only a square of concrete left to indicate that a home had even been there. The homes that remained uninhabitable had X's spray painted inside circles, and in each section was a number or blank, meaning the number of lives lost. Antebellum homes were torn up or gone. Ultimately, it took more than ten years for the coast to return to a normal we could all recognize and be comfortable with. Some of the restaurants were destroyed, some returned, and some relocated.

When I returned home, I turned in my two-week notice at work and started packing. On May 8, my boys kissed me goodbye. They sent their momma on her way to a better life and a greater love, not that there wouldn't be heartaches with being away from my boys and lifelong friends. But I would be near my parents again, which worked for me. So, at 3:00 a.m., I hit the road to new adventures and a love that had just been a dream a few weeks before. It finally occurred to both of us that this was really happening.

I later arrived at Robby's house in Lizana, Mississippi. He had left the house key for me to leave my belongings. Truthfully, as I walked through his house, I realized the devastation the hurricane had caused in Lizana, too, just seventeen miles north of the coast. As I walked through it, I almost got back in my car and sped westwards as fast as possible. Thank God I didn't listen to my head and heard what my heart was screaming:

stay.

I drove to downtown Gulfport and found Robby organizing his new office building and dealing with AT&T. I entered the door, but he didn't hear it open. But when I walked around the corner, he hung up the phone and smiled, his whole face lighting up with his love for me. I had never seen a man look at me like he did. It was as if his feelings shone a light over his whole body.

"Let's go," he said. "We gotta get a ring on that finger before some old beau finds out you're back in town."

We spent the next two hours searching for the right ring. I picked one on a billboard and told him, "No, not that one. Everyone in town will be wearing that one."

On May 10, we took our first road trip together to move the rest of my large household items to his house and celebrate us. Vickie, a sister from another mister, helped me set up everything at our hotel. We had a cake topper, chilled champagne, cheese, crackers, and many other goodies. It was a six-hour drive back to Texas, and we talked and laughed the whole way.

On May 11, we headed to San Antonio and found a B&B in New Braunfels, surrounded by many little shops. We walked in and out of every store and around the town, holding hands, enjoying each other after all the lost time, and realizing that we loved each other as deeply now as we ever had. Our hearts were still connected, and our hands and feet always found each other's.

That evening, we drove to the riverwalk in San Antonio. A canal surrounds the riverwalk. There are restaurants, shops, hotels, and a mall along the canal. Robby spotted a Zales jewelry store in the mall, so he took my hand and guided me, not telling me where we were going. When we walked in, he asked for the bridal selection. Walking over to the display, he pointed out a ring and asked me to try it on. He had remembered one that caught my eye in Biloxi the week before. I hadn't asked to try it on because it was pretty pricey.

"Are you sure?" I asked.

"Just put it on, and let's see."

The ring had an intricate platinum setting that stood tall and would catch the attention of passersby. When I put it on, it looked like that ring had been made for my hand, and it looked like it had been on my finger for twenty years. I cried, and he asked why. I told him that the way it looked with the tall setting reminded me of the ironwork on the Mississippi River Bridge that I had been driving over for twenty-two years to return home. It was meant to be.

Later that evening, I excused myself to use the restroom at dinner. When I returned, Robby got down on one knee and proposed. Not one of my other husbands had ever proposed like that. Everyone in the restaurant cheered, and (of course) I cried. That was the beginning of a fantastic weekend and life together.

From that moment on, Robby and I were inseparable—except for when he was at work, which was more than an hour's drive one way. While he was at work, I dealt with the contractors who were finishing up our Katrina-damaged house. I also planned our wedding and cared for his girls during the weeks we had them.

It was summer now, and softball was in full swing by then. Rumors and questions about me, my reputation, and my intentions with Robby were going around, and his ex-wife was involved in them. I found myself dodging lies and hurtful comments from her friends and family. His girls came home from school and cornered me in the camper kitchen (one way in and one way out).

"So, we have been told you have twelve kids and have been married and divorced fourteen times." All I could say was, "Well, if I had twelve kids, I would really like to know where the other ten are because I would never have run out on my kids, and no, I have not been married fourteen times, four yes, not fourteen so go back and tell whoever told you these lies that they need to come to me for the true story and stop telling lies about people they don't know."

The wedding was coming along nicely. Robby insisted that I wear a white gown, even though I was forty and had married and divorced more than once. White was not what I had planned, but he said he was making a wrong right and wanted the wedding to be what I had always wanted. So, I had to go shopping.

I found a gown at a local bridal shop. Trying it on, I found it fit like it had been custom-fitted just for me—just like the ring. A week later, Robby asked how the dress shopping was going. I told him I thought I found one, but it was over seven hundred dollars.

"It's just money, babe. Go get it," was his response. Then he asked me to describe it. When I went online to find it, the dress popped up in an online magazine for more than a thousand dollars.

"Babe," he said, "that is fate. Let's go right now."

When we drove to the store, they still had it. The shop owner said she had put it in the back because no one else would fit it like I did. She just knew I would be back.

On the way back home, Robby went with me to shop for invitations, tableware, napkins, and decorations. We also picked out and ordered food items. A cousin made our three-tiered cake, pearl white with red roses cascading and swirling down so they could be seen from all sides. We picked out table linens and flatware. We found an altar. Robby also helped me pick out the flowers I would use for bouquets and to decorate the altar.

For his wedding outfit, Robby chose black jeans instead of dress slacks. After all, it was an outdoor wedding with BBQ, gumbo, and brisket, which my aunt (Momma) would cook for us. We also picked out a white dress shirt with black onyx pearl buttons and a maroon paisley vest. My maids of honor were wearing flowy pant suits and would hold red rose bouquets that I would make personally.

On Saturday, October 21, at 2:00 p.m. at my Paw Paw's home, where I grew up, I became Mrs. Robby Osborne. It was the happiest day of my life, next to giving birth to my two sons. What was funny was that no one knew we had already been married for two months! Back to the rumors about me and my character.

Robby came home one day after I had attempted to explain all of the malicious lies to his daughters that his ex-wife had created. Frustrated, I told him we get married now, or I am calling this whole thing off.

"We're raising girls and living together out of wedlock, and I will not be your live-in girlfriend much longer!"

I wasn't sure what his reaction would be, so I was prepared to pack everything again and head back west. But Robby took me in his arms and told me to pick a date.

"Tell me what time and where I need to be." So, on July 25, we were married by a fantastic Christian Justice of the Peace in Gulfport, Mississippi. No one knew any better, so when his ex-wife and her mother threatened to crash our wedding, I had the privilege of telling them both that we were already married and that my cousin, the Sheriff Deputy (now the Sheriff), would also be there in uniform waiting to take them to jail for trespassing.

"So, I dare you."

I made the mistake of allowing Robby to plan the honeymoon. He and my dad were in cahoots on this one. My dad called me and told me that I would need a passport if I were planning on being a part of the honeymoon, so I had to order my birth certificate for that to happen. Then, when it came in, my dad told me all I needed to do was go to vital records and pick it up. When it arrived, I got excited. I hadn't been back to Hawaii since I was one year old.

We got in the car two days after our wedding, and Robby started driving east. Knowing you couldn't drive to Hawaii, I asked him how long we had to drive there.

"We're going to the Caribbean," he said.

Well, I knew we couldn't drive there either, so being the insistent person I am, I pestered him until he finally gave in.

"OK, we're going to the Disney World Caribbean resort."

What the hell? I wasted $100 on passport fees and $50 on birth certificates! But I quickly got over it because I had never been to Disney before.

Robby gave me many firsts and wonderfully beautiful memories during our eleven years of marriage. Before Robby found me, my life could be summed up by the word "wrong." Wrong husbands, wrong friends, just flat-out wrong. The only good thing that was going for me was my boys. But in the romance department, somehow,

I would always find the person who talked down to me, swore at me, cheated on me, and hit me.

One of these men slapped me so hard across the face that I rolled several feet across the front yard. Most of them lied to me, hid important things from me, and gaslighted me. They always left me feeling like I had done something wrong. I must have. Otherwise, why would they treat me so cruelly? I had given 1000% to every relationship, never getting a small fraction back. One can only give so much before they are done, which is why I have been married more than a couple of times. I will give someone a million chances as long as they are honestly trying. But I am gone when I see that you are just playing with my emotions. And I don't give second chances once I leave.

One day, as I walked out the door to get diapers and formula for our infant son, my first husband told me that if I did my hair and makeup, I might find another husband. But I didn't need to fix my hair or makeup, and that was all it took for me to realize that five very long, emotionally abusive years was too long for anyone to bear. I didn't deserve that. Before that, he always stayed late with his Army buddies and ran the road without telling who. Every other day, he told me he wanted a divorce. So, six months later, I finally stopped crying.

"Okay, you got it." I was done.

Because I didn't have anyone I could trust, he talked me into using the exact attorney to save money for the divorce, and I ended up not getting paramount custody of my kids. This taught me much about his character, my own, and my trust in everyone. Even though we shared joint custody, he had paramount custody over the boys. So, he controlled them and me.

For example, when it was my weekend, he would tell me he had plans with them and ask if we could switch. What he was telling them, however, was that I didn't want them anymore and didn't love them. To this day, he still plays games with them and everyone else in his life. But if he was not in a relationship with another woman, I was the best mother on the planet. He had my boys so confused that when my youngest was only eight, he thought I had never been in his life until then. But I was the one who took him to family birthday parties and baseball games! I was at every ball game and every play, and they made yearly road trips to my family home in Mississippi! But that goes to show just how deep emotional abuse hits children. My son suppressed memories because of the abuse.

Not only did the abuse affect my youngest son, but it also involved my oldest as well. He was afraid to ask me to take them from their dad because he knew his brother wanted to be with his dad. And he couldn't leave his brother behind.

Then there was a cocaine-addicted husband who tried to rape me when he insisted on hand-delivering our divorce papers. Then, there was an alcoholic husband who swung a baseball bat at my head for dumping out a hot beer. Then, there was the slapper.

I had been divorced for five years when Robby found me. That's not to say that I didn't see any more losers during that time because I did—I just didn't marry them. It seemed at the time that I could pick the biggest loser out of the largest crowd in Texas. But Robby found me at a high point when I had some confidence back, had a good job, paid my way through school, and practiced massage therapy at a few chiropractors' offices. I was doing good.

When Robby and I took our first road trip, we compared lives for six hours, wondering how we were still alive and didn't have some disease. It was only God's will that protected us through it all. He was always there for us both, and it didn't take us long to realize He was all over our finding each other when we did. Things just clicked, not in any way we had clicked through on our own. He took care of the meeting, the planning, and the follow-through, but Robby took care of the ending all by himself.

We had our issues in the beginning. His ex refused to allow us to be at peace and always caused us grief. But we stayed tightly together, leaning on each other and our God. In eleven years, we married each other three times: first by a Justice of the Peace, second by renewing our vows three months later at our big wedding, and again in 2013 when Robby joined the Catholic church.

On every anniversary and birthday, we took a week to go to resorts to reconnect and celebrate. We decided to put in a pool at our home, our new vacation destination. But Robby needed to be farther away from his office. He always wanted to be at work, even when it was our vacation, so I quickly vetoed his staycations. On the third renewal, he surprised me with a trip back to Honolulu: ten days of just us on the beaches, visiting where I was born, learning about the rights I had been born with because I was born in The Queens Hospital. I am entitled to local discounts and rent—not the ninety-nine-year, one-dollar rent, but a drastic discount.

Robby made every vacation pleasant. One

year, we took his girls to Fiesta Texas, a theme park by Six Flags. We pulled our fifth-wheel travel trailer for more than ten hours to spend a week there. And every morning, he surprised me with my favorite Starbucks coffee in bed. He was so faithful about the Starbucks coffee that I eventually had to have emergency surgery to remove a kidney stone that was more than double the size of my urethra tube! He told me that he had never prayed so hard for anyone and had never been so terrified that I would not make it. We learned that I was born with a defective urethra tube. The area where it splits from the kidney to the bladder is smaller than the rest of the tube, and that is where the stone is lodged. I only had about twelve hours of warning signs. And with being jerked back and forth by the travel trailer, I needed to figure out the issue quickly!

Robby was always spoiling me with lovely gifts for no reason—only because he could and always wanted to. We always worked, laughed, played, traveled, planned, and shed tears together, and we held hands doing it all (it did not matter who was watching).

However, when our surveying business started slowing down in 2014, it sent Robby into a downward spiral. That was when he began talking again about how the Osborne men didn't live beyond age 50. He was starting to retreat within himself and picking fights with me over nothing at all.

He found another land survey company that was older and much more established than ours. He asked me what I thought about buying it to supplement our income. I suggested we pray over it to see what God would show us. We were always faithful to our Christianity by tithing, giving, and volunteering. We knew the Lord would be as faithful to us as He had always been.

It was Thanksgiving when nine of our family members met us at Disney. Everyone was having a great time, or so I thought. For one, Robby's daughter had a "huge secret" she was threatening to spill. Second, Robby was picking fights with me in front of a few family members, so much so that I had to excuse myself from Thanksgiving dinner. And if that wasn't enough, he followed me to the restroom and threatened me, which floored me. Robby had never done that before, and I could not wrap my head around why he was acting so mean. After all, Robby was not a mean person.

What had I done? In recent years, our success had changed him. He had become more boastful and showy, acting as if he had succeeded by himself and as if I played no role in it. He would verbally attack me if I said or did anything he perceived took credit away from him. Robby prohibited me from making toasts at dinners or taking any credit for anything. The night of our Thanksgiving dinner, he stated that this was the best Thanksgiving he had ever had. When I mentioned that I had cooked every holiday meal for more than fifty family members, including his large family, he said, "I don't remember you doing any of that." When I mentioned it to Nan-Nan, she stated he must have been celebrating the holidays somewhere else because "You have done all of the holidays since you moved back from Texas."

A horrible storm happened in December 2016, just two weeks before Christmas. Houses around us caught fire from lightning, and the sounds of tornadoes surrounded us. As he left across the pond to check on Robby's mom, our house went stark white, as if enveloped in a world of white light. The generator kicked on. It was running, but the transformer blew up. All those surges kept going on and off and through the generator for a loop. In the end, lightning had sneaked through, hit our sleep number bed, and caught it on fire. I was dealing with a house fire, and I could see that Robby was freaking out again. He was so terrified that I could have died and that he had not been there to protect me.

A week passed, and we dealt with the fire's aftermath with repairs, dry-cleaning trips, bills, and battling the insurance company. That was when I really noticed that Robby started changing. He was so tunnel-visioned with his own problems that he could not see that I needed help and could not know that it had deeply affected me. I was emotionally and physically exhausted by mid-January, and he was still changing for the worse. He started losing weight, and his blood pressure was soaring. But he refused to get help. I was dealing with him, me, our business, the kids, and my parents, and there was no time for me to heal.

On December 26, 2016, Robby started accusing me of cheating on him. By that point, there was nothing to do but begin marriage counseling. In therapy, I learned that he assumed I had a large secret to keep because he had seen me crying in church. He could not understand that all the stress from the fights, his verbal threats, and how rapidly he was changing into someone I didn't recognize was scaring the hell out of me. He apologized for the accusation and for his behavior, and I thought we were good.

By March 2017, Robby had decided to buy the surveying company and asked me if I would cosign it. When I said no, something flipped like a switch inside Robby, and from then on, I could not reach him like I used to. He was already gone, picking fights with me as he was leaving for work, not spending time alone with me anymore, and changing passwords to his phones and devices (he never used to have one before). I had lost a fight and didn't know I needed to fight.

On April 15 (Tax Day), we met with our attorney and the other business owner to sign papers. I have never seen anyone sign papers so fast as I did that day. But before the final page was signed, I saw Robby hesitate. It was the promissory note page, stating that no matter what, he promised to continue payments until the whole $400,000 was paid. A naturally dark-complected man, his skin went white as a ghost. But even before the attorneys could explain the meaning of the last page to them, Robby and the other business owner had them signed. It was done.

He left that day smiling, and I thought he was going to be okay and that he was coming back to me. But this was the beginning of the end, and somewhere deep inside, I could feel something was still off.

On Monday morning, Robby dressed, left me with a kiss, and told me he loved me and would check on me when he got a chance. We had not worked apart since we started his business in 2006 on his fortieth birthday. Watching him drive away, I felt my world had stopped.

He called me at lunch and asked if I would come down and try to organize the office for him. When I arrived, I saw a different man than the one who had left home a few hours before.

"I made a huge mistake," Robby said. He was bright red from high blood pressure. When I asked what was wrong, he told me that the new business he purchased operated like a sweatshop and that he never got a break. I could tell he was overwhelmed and stressed, probably because the man who sold him the business insisted that he "stay in the background," which was unnecessary because Robby could do it, especially with me behind him.

Each time I visited the new office, I saw less and less of Robby. He was always too busy even to sit for a second with me. He was losing weight at a rapid pace, and his face stayed bright red. He was also sleeping less, and when he did, he snored fiercely.

Now, the licensed holder for two large surveying firms, he has done all the Q&As for both and signed every project. Sometimes, he worked until midnight and would be up again at 4:00 a.m. He would even work Saturdays and Sundays if I allowed it.

Not sleeping, not eating, staying stressed out, and feeling beat down by the business partner, not only was Robby suffering, but I constantly stayed worried for his health and sanity. He began talking about the Osborne curse again, but it was hard for me to pull him out of it this time.

-------------**STAKE IT!**-------------

QUESTION: *If you have a blended family, on a scale of 1 to 5, how well do you fit in?*

CONSIDERATION: Please, refer to the section on independence in Chapter 5's STAKE IT!

CHALLENGE: Repeat Chapter 5's challenge. This time, ask your partner to do something about it.

ABOVE: Robby in the summer of 2107 just two months before he died. He's standing outside a home he had just finished surveying before it was auctioned off for $3.5 million. This is the last photo I had of him before his death. BELOW: This was the "Hard Thanksgiving" at Disney the year before Robby died, when everything went wrong.

CHAPTER 7
The Beginning of the End

July 3rd started as a usual Monday morning. The next day would be my aunt's birthday. Nothing special was planned for this year since the kids would not be home, so we planned to cook burgers for her by the pool and relax. Years before, it would have been a blowout party, as our family always celebrated our annual family reunion on her birthday until Paw Paw passed away in 1992. We did not do that again until my dad's seventy-fifth birthday. Robby and I were blessed to have over one hundred fifty family and friends at our home. What a weekend that was! Wyatt was eleven months old and loved all the attention. He spent most of his afternoon in his great-grandpa's lab, enjoying whatever anyone gave him to eat. They both slept great that night.

At 6:00 a.m. the morning after (a Monday) Robby "flipped a switch" again, sat on the edge of the bed, and started rocking back and forth. His eyes were glossed over, his skin was pale white, and he was drooling uncontrollably out of the right corner of his mouth. I panicked, thinking that he was having a stroke. He was not verbal, just rocking. When I touched him, he turned to look at me, but he looked right through me as if I wasn't even there. When he finally started trying to speak, he only spoke a few words and was lethargic.

As I sat and held his hand, tears started to roll down his cheek.

"I'm losing my mind, but I cannot go to the ER. They will take my license away." He kept saying that over and over.

Robby was so proud of what he and we had accomplished in the world of land surveying. He had made an excellent reputation for himself even before I arrived, and everyone looked up to him for advice on land issues and even on drafting blueprints for their homes. I was proud of him and us. We have come a long way since April 2006.

As I touched him again after he told me he

would lose his license, all I could think to say was, "We will get through this together, just like everything else life has thrown our way. Side by side, holding hands, and crazy about each other."

With those words, he seemed to return to me, like the bad dream he was living suddenly turned off. He got up, showered, and dressed. Before he left, he hugged me tight and kissed me like it was the first kiss we shared after twenty-two years. But that morning, the tears I cried weren't from arguing with Robby, which had been happening a lot lately. They were tears of fear. Fear for him and me not being with him throughout the day. Fear for us. Where are we going? How did we get here? How will we get through this?

Robby attended a seminar with some local realtors, where he spoke. He called me to tell me it went well when the seminar was over. Other realtors asked him to speak at their next meeting, too. He was on a mission to educate realtors about why it is vital to have their clients complete a land survey before selling or buying any property.

Robby talked to Mike (his business partner) to get advice about how he keeps from losing his mind with all the work required to run his two businesses. Mike told him to sit down with the stacks of paperwork and complete one page at a time. Once you finish one page, then move on to the following page and the next. Before you realize it, your stack is gone, and you are still breathing and moving on to something else.

When Robby got home, we enjoyed dinner and a glass of wine. He didn't go to my office that night. We just sat, talked, and even soaked in the tub together without discussing work. The next day was relaxing, too. Then, we could restart ourselves and make different plans for the future.

Surprisingly, Robby asked me to call our family doctor and ask for antidepressants and sleeping pills. Dr. Stephen Schepens is our age and has been Robby's doctor for over twenty years. They knew each other well, like friends. When I moved back, he became my doctor as well.

When I called Doc, he called back almost immediately. He knew something was wrong with Robby because he wouldn't even take a Tylenol. Doc was worried. The next afternoon, we went to see him, and he spent nearly an hour talking to Robby about everything that was happening, trying to make sure that Robby knew what he was asking for and understood the side effects. In the end, we left with three prescriptions: Lexapro for antidepressants, Xanax for anxiety, and Ambien for sleep. He told Robby not to drive or make major decisions after taking the sleeping pill in the evening.

Robby started the meds the next day. When he woke up the next morning, he looked like a little kid, having slept all night for the first time in months. I told him that was a good sign because I didn't sleep a wink with him snoring so loud. I had to go outside the room for peace and quiet, but I could still hear him. He laughed.

The next evening, he took the sleeping pills again. This time, however, he said he didn't sleep at all. I had to reassure him that he did, and I didn't because of his snoring. This went on until the very end.

Most of our morning fights from that point on were about Robby saying how he was sleep-deprived and exhausted when, in fact, it was I who was sleep-deprived and exhausted beyond belief. But there was no way to get Robby to realize what the Ambien was doing to him, which was one of the side effects: making people do and feel unthinkable things when they are genuinely sound asleep. Some people have murdered, driven cars, shopped, and raped while under the influence of these pharmaceuticals. They have done things they would never do in their right mind.

So, we were back at our morning routine, arguing, and I was being unconsoled by my usually loving, tender husband. I was at my wits' end again, picking up the pieces of his train wreck again, wondering what I had done to make him hate me every single morning. Not only was I emotionally a wreck, but I had no one to talk to anymore. Robby had been my best friend for eleven beautiful years. Now, I had no one.

On Wednesday, September 13, I told Robby I needed a break and wanted to see my friend Shelley in Nashville, Tennessee. That night was date night (Wednesday), and we would do whatever we wanted. Usually, we had steak at Captain Al's on the water. Sometimes, we did dinner and walked through Sam's Club, window shopping, and holding hands. This evening, it was a family therapy appointment for anxiety and depression. Doc did not like the results that Robby was having and didn't feel comfortable giving him refills anymore, so he made Robby see a therapist.

At 6:00 p.m., we walked into the clinic. It started getting dark outside, but it was warm and friendly. We met with his therapist, who watched us closely when we sat. She commented that we were in love and asked about our story. Robby told her he had been searching the internet for my name for years and finally found me and brought me back home. Then she asked why we were in her office. After giving her our answers, she gave us both homework for the next week. She said she also wanted me to get into therapy for my marriage and for the personal abuse I experienced during my childhood.

As we left, Robby kissed me and told me how sorry he was for everything. He promised to work hard to get us back to where we were. We drove to the beach, sat in the sand, and talked for hours. We were in separate cars, so he followed me home when we left.

The following day, Robby picked yet another fight. I told him I would see Shelley the next day, September 15, and that I needed a break to clear my head and breathe again. He asked if he could come.

"Of course, but what would that solve? I will work on my homework, and you will work on yours."

Friday, Robby kissed me goodbye, told me he loved me, and texted me throughout the day. I was so confused. How could he go from fighting with me and having no communication to talking to me constantly and then start playing games with me in the evening? I went to bed crying, feeling so alone. Shelley consoled me, telling me she didn't know what to think. His behavior shocked her, and she told me it would be better on Monday when I returned. We just needed some time apart.

Saturday, Robby made me angry every chance he got. He would text, asking me a question while working on his homework, and then he would go MIA for hours, to the point that a neighbor had to check on him for me to ensure he was okay. The person I called found him aimlessly looking at the pond on the front porch. They had talked and laughed like always, so he assumed Robby was okay.

By Sunday morning, I had written fifteen pages of my homework, front and back, while Robby said he had written twenty-five. We discussed the new Pirates of the Caribbean movie coming out and wondered how Disney would implement that into their ride in Florida, which was Robby's all-time favorite!

When I woke up on September 18 to drive back home, I never would have imagined the nightmare I was about to enter. Robby had promised never to do this to me, our kids, or our parents. But when I look back, it seems to me that he was not promising he would not kill himself. He was promising he would not kill himself inside our home and leave a mess for me to clean up like several others in our community had. We had always talked about how they could leave such a mess for someone you love to have to clean up when you are gone. In the end, he kept that promise, just not the promise that he made to me eleven years ago when I left my life in Texas behind to marry him.

There were so many things happening the night Robby passed. There were so many loving people and so many hurt souls who were left behind to wonder what drove Robby to hurt himself and to pick up the pieces he nearly destroyed with one pull of the trigger.

One of my high school friends and employees found him around 7:30 a.m. Robby was lying on his side when John saw him. John thought he had a heartache. But when he rolled Robby over, the gun fell out of his mouth. John panicked, called Allan to help him, and then called his wife, a dear friend of mine and Shelley's.

I felt so alone when Shelley and I drove home. My boys were now eleven years older. Both had been in the military and were now out. My youngest, Jim, was now married with two handsome sons. His older son, Wyatt, was now three, and Ben would be two in a few months.

When everyone woke up the morning after,

Jim and his wife, Tifeni, walked over from where they had been staying, and little Wyatt came running. Still timid, Nana and little Ben started running. But when I hugged Wyatt, he stopped. It took him a while to realize I was his Nana too, that he could come running anytime he wanted, and that I would love on him just the same.

So many people came to check on me, bring food, and give out hugs throughout the day. However, I still had a business to run, people who needed to be paid, questions that had to be answered, and decisions that had to be made. I was already hearing rumors from the family that Robby's ex-wife and daughters were already setting appointments with attorneys to take everything from me that was "rightfully theirs." Robby had yet to be gone twenty-eight hours before Hell opened, and I was being pushed into it. Life without Robby was not what I had asked for. I had moved back to Lizana, Mississippi, to have my forever with the love of my life. Not this.

The first night, I went to bed with B on one side snoring and my sister Angie on the other: three women sleeping in a queen-sized bed with barely enough room to breathe, much less rollover. At one point, I was crying, and my sister, so sweetly, just hugged me tightly and let me cry it out. B's snoring made me miss Robby. Regardless of how loud and disturbing his snoring was, I wanted him back, but that would never come again.

No more morning fights, no more soaking in the tub, no more date nights, no more walks along the beach, no more battles to see who would be the first to say "Happy Anniversary" ever again, and no more little scar under that sky-blue eye.

All week long, I had meetings with attorneys, therapists, church leaders, and clergy to arrange his memorial and set a time for our final viewing before he was to be cremated, which I got called "a greedy bitch" for doing. Little did his daughters know at the time that cremation was what Robby wanted and that he wanted his ashes to be spread under the Golden Gate Bridge in San Francisco like his brother David and his father's mom. Instead, we split his ashes. They each got some, and so did his mother. The rest was buried on top of his dad's grave, where Robby would always visit when he was upset.

The memorial was held in our tiny hometown Catholic church, St. Ann's Catholic Church in Lizana, Mississippi, at 10:00 a.m. Mass would start at 11:00 a.m., and his life would be remembered afterward at our home. One of his daughters put together a slideshow of their favorite photos, including funny videos of him and me playing the dance-off on the Wii. They also made us all jersey shirts with the LA Raiders logo, which was his favorite sports team, and they printed on the back where the name was supposed to go, whatever we called him.

Robby's favorite band was ACDC, and they played "Back in Black" at the house. We all laughed and then cried. Over three hundred people were at the church service. Some had to be turned away because of fire safety rules. There were so many stories and memories. And then his business "partner" showed up.

"You need to honor his reputation and do the right thing," he said to me, meaning that I needed to pay the promissory note (which I did not).

"Sell the business," I told him. "I'm not paying a damn thing! He destroyed his reputation when he shot himself!"

Later, when I told my dad what he had said, my father told me I should have pointed him out. Being a retired Police Chief at the local SEABEE base, my father would have thrown him out of the church. Thankfully, this man got the message because he never showed his face again. He did put a block on the bank account, but I took back some of the money I had loaned Robby to buy the new business before he did that.

I ensured the employees were paid on Friday and Saturday mornings at 10:00 a.m. at the church where the community fell in love with Robby. We said goodbye. We shared many stories, tears, and laughter at his celebration of life at our house. It's funny that at 51 years old, your entire life is celebrated in just a matter of hours. Then, those pieces are formed into something we once knew. *How do you piece life together without someone so important to you, your kids, and your existence? Am I allowed to make all these decisions that everyone wants answers to? Why do they act like the answer is needed right now?*

That is how the next several weeks went for me: the beginning of the end. With answers being forced out of me and no one to bounce them off, I could call Jarod. God knows that he was my lifeline that first week and still was. Jarod is my cousin, but more like my twin from another lifetime. We are so much alike that it's scary. He could read my eyes and know if I was telling the truth about my sanity or lying to survive another day. He would start my days by sending me a text. Then he would call me on FaceTime if he heard something that he didn't like. By the end of the call, I would be okay again. And then he would call with his usual humor, "This is your welfare check," every evening just to see how my day went. He, Jesus, my family, and close friends kept me planted on this planet.

------------STAKE IT!------------

QUESTION: *On a scale of 1 to 5, how much of your self-worth, needs, and concerns do you feel are allowed to be expressed in your current relationship?*

CONSIDERATION: It's important to recognize warning signs and listen to your gut instincts as your primary navigational guides, especially when the real possibility exists of a partner hurting themselves or you. Actually, you must remain vigilant for indicators of destructive behaviors within your partnership—without being paranoid. These warning signs may include patterns of manipulation, withdrawal, a lack of drive, verbal or physical aggression, or little to no respect for boundaries.

Surrounding yourself with a supportive network of friends, family, or professionals also can be like a safety net when things get more difficult in the relationship. Similar to a team of surveyors providing guidance and assistance on a challenging projects, a supportive community offers kindness, validation, perspective, and practical assistance. This network can also offer emotional support, practical advice, and access to resources like counseling or legal assistance, empowering you to make informed decisions and take necessary steps to protect yourself and your partner.

In situations where the safety and well-being of yourself or others are at risk, seeking legal protection is a must. In the extreme end of things, this may involve obtaining restraining orders, seeking legal counsel for divorce or separation proceedings, or taking legal action to ensure accountability for harmful behaviors. Legal protections establish clear boundaries and consequences for destructive actions. In many cases, it can also be a deterrent.

By recognizing warning signs, trusting intuition, fostering a supportive network, and seeking legal protection when necessary, you can be empowered to prioritize your safety and well-being, fostering healthier, more fulfilling partnerships built on mutual respect and trust.

CHALLENGE: Do a "buddy check" with your partner. (A buddy check is a mutual agreement between partners to regularly check in with each other for safety, well-being, and emotional support).

LEFT: Rascal at about four weeks old. He had separation anxiety one day, so he climbed up my leg and onto the bed that I was making up, just to get close to me. He was orphaned at two weeks old when his momma died. RIGHT: Rascal at eight weeks old as my navigator and trying to keep me from turning into the vet's office for his checkup and shot. You can't see it, but he has one blue eye and one green eye and is a smaller Maine Coon mix. He gets credit for comforting me in the middle of the night when I would have night terrors, and he saved me several times when it was too late to call my boys or besties. Sometimes, it's just nice to have another living soul to remind you that life does go on and not to quit.

CHAPTER 8

New Beginnings

There were days I wanted to end the battle, but some things kept me going. There were days when I thought people were making this shit up to keep me here, and then there were days when I didn't know or feel much of anything so that I wanted to end my own life. I was going through the motions, begging God to explain why Robby did this, why he left me, why he lied to me, and why it hurt so much.

Six months before Robby's death, I had a dream. I was walking through rolling sands, like the Sahara Desert. Up ahead of me in the far distance, I could see a figure, not sure man or woman, and they didn't seem to be moving away from me. Still, they were moving their feet, but I was the only one actually moving. As I got closer, I saw that the person had long, warm, sandy blonde hair full of curls and was wearing a robe with a rope belt tied. I was not sure if he was wearing sandals or barefoot, but as I got within arms reach, the person turned around, and the face I saw was Jesus. He didn't speak words, but I heard him say, "Come, follow me."

I didn't understand the dream. I only understood it to mean that Jesus wanted me to start following him more diligently like I had years before when we weren't practicing Catholicism. I forgot about this dream but remembered it from time to time, and when Robby died, it all came to me. He was warning me, He knew what Robby was thinking, He wanted me to be prepared for a dark period in my life, and I knew I was still loved and cared for.

Before Robby passed, we had planned a vacation for the next month. Shelley, Shelley's husband Paul, and their son Cole had already paid for their tickets. We were supposed to be staying at one of our vacation villas, so all they had to do was pay for their airfare and meals. The villa was taken care of by our vacation plan. When he passed, I couldn't get a refund or a credit for him, so our friend Selma took his place. When it was time for me to go on Robby's favorite ride, I had a panic attack and ran out of line to breathe.

New Beginnings

Shelley and Selma both held my hands and hugged me hard so I could get through it. Once that episode ended, I put on my big girl panties, marched back to the ride, and rode it like a boss.

I would be rich if I had a penny for every rumor that flew around while I was at Disney. She's cheating. She's partying. She doesn't care. She didn't miss a beat. Someone started the rumor that I wasn't with Shelley the weekend Robby passed: I was with another man. Even when they questioned Shelley, they still didn't believe either of us. But everyone needed to blame someone. It couldn't be Robby's fault. He would never do this. She drove him to this. She beat him. He beat her. None of these things could have been farther from the truth.

I had so many weeks on end of night terrors. I remember one night bolting out of bed, cursing and screaming at God, "You promised that 'ask and you shall receive!'" I had been asking for the night terrors to be removed from me for months, and they were just getting worse. I wasn't sleeping, I wasn't eating. My dad and godfather showed up a couple of times a month to drag me out of the house to ensure I had at least one good meal. I would shut the gate and lock it tight at 2:30 pm every afternoon. I didn't want to be bothered.

My cousin, Joyce Nicole Ladner Dees (January 24, 1983 – March 12, 2023), once told me, "I knew you would reach out when you were ready—not a moment before—so I left you alone."

Even the employees, who now were all my responsibility, needed to vent their anger for what Robby had done to someone. I became their whipping post at times. About nine months into our grieving period (in all honesty, there wasn't one), I took some time alone after everyone had left for home, drove to my cousin Jarod's house, and stayed with him for a week. I used his house to hide from the world so no one could bother me. After being there for a while, I realized that Selma, who had been working by herself answering phones, dealing with clients, collecting money, making deposits, and even working in the field, hadn't gotten paid! When it hit me, and I contacted her, all she said was, "That is what friends do. We step in when you cannot, and we step up."

Nine months into this, I showed up at the office parking lot one morning to a surprise. There was no place for anyone, much less a client, to park. The large white diesel work truck and trailer that carried all the equipment to the jobs were backed up to the front door. I walked in very calmly (though I felt other than calm inside), found Allan, and asked him to park the truck somewhere else because no one had a place to park.

Usually angry with me for something or other, Allan was calm and relaxed. However, since Robby died, it felt as though he was trying to take Robby's place as lead authority. He even went as far as asking me for the profit and loss report one day.

"I want to make sure we are making a profit."

"Did you pay about two hundred and fifty thousand dollars to buy the company?"

"No."

"No? Then why in the hell would you think I would allow you to see that? The profit and loss is my concern and no one else's."

On the same day as the parking incident, I sent out a group text telling everyone who worked in the field and drove a large vehicle to start parking in the grass on top of the hill about fifty feet from the front door so that all other smaller cars could park in their usual spot. The situation ended up causing a major ordeal. Within minutes, I had a text from Allan demanding a meeting at 4:00 p.m. I told him that I was home in bed with a severe migraine and that it would have to wait until tomorrow morning. But he insisted.

I got up against my will, went to the office, and he started in on me like I was his employee and had committed a crime against the company.

"Well, just where would you like to park?" he asked sarcastically.

"I don't care where I park, but my clients will have a clear spot whenever they arrive and at all times." He tried to tell me he was told not to park on the grass. I reminded him that the person who told him that was no longer here and to follow my instructions.

The following day, the mood was very heavy. I called a meeting before anyone left the office, even though Allan tried to tell me they were leaving anyway. I informed him he could leave and never return if that was what he wanted. I quickly reminded him that he would never have spoken to Robby like that and that I demanded the same respect.

He brought up the profit and loss report again.

"When I have a check for two hundred and fifty grand in my bank account, you can see all the profit and loss reports you want, but until then, don't bring it up again."

"You know I don't have to work here," he shot back.

"And neither do I, but I don't see Robby making sure that your paycheck doesn't bounce every two weeks or that you all have work for next week. But feel free to go home if you like, Allan. But when you return, make sure you know who the boss is because it's not you." As painful as it was, I had to remind the employees that Robby did this to all of us and that we all needed to get on the same page or close the doors. Because it was just us now, all the rules that Robby had set into place no longer existed.

Before they left for the day, I told Allan that he no longer had personal access to the diesel work truck and that it was to be parked in the yard at the end of the day with the gate locked and the keys left in the office.

A few months into the process, Allan asked if he could move into Robby's old office. I told him that I didn't mind. But it didn't take long for him to make me feel like he was spying on me. Anytime I had someone visit, he would call me and ask who it was or why they were there, which mainly happened on weekends when no one else was there. I quickly reeled him back in and stopped allowing him to work on days when no one else was there. I also told him my yard was no one's concern or business unless I was harmed.

I often got left out of meetings and constantly had to remind people that I was the sole owner of SSG. Meetings were to occur with me present, no matter the reason. I reminded them that they included Robby in all meetings and decision-making, and so should they include me. Several people had my back, and I eventually had to remind myself they were not out to get me and take everything left. The company and I were in good hands. Life without Robby helping me navigate these waters was no longer an option, and I had to trust the people who were still with me or shut it all down and walk away.

In the end, six years later, I had to take a long, hard look at how things were operating and realize that we weren't getting the work we used to. I remember Robby saying many years ago that our most important client only kept one sub for ten years. We had been there for seventeen years, so that it may be time. After we completed our last Annual Volume Ash survey, I called a meeting with all of their department heads and announced it was time to say goodbye. I thanked them profusely for the years and the kindness they all showed me when Robby passed away. We shed some tears and laughs, and we went our separate ways.

On August 28, 2023, I completed my last quarterly return, called my CPA, and announced what was happening. He agreed it was time to stop the financial bleeding because SSG was now in my account for more than three hundred thousand dollars.

When Robby passed, his company still owed me more than thirty-two thousand. I just couldn't do it anymore. No one was bailing me out or checking on me to ensure I could eat and pay my bills. I needed to stop being that for others.

In May 2023, I closed on the sale of my house. I sold it to a warm and caring couple who had no idea of the tragedy that had taken place at their new home just six years before. One year later, they told me they also wanted to buy the rental house that used to be our office and became an Airbnb. It was time for my heart and soul to complete this healing process.

There will always be something negative that follows a good, better, or your "best" day. No matter what reason, and regardless of the amount of love in a relationship, people must and will blame someone. But in the end, there is healing. From the memories. From other people. From talking about the past with kind people who don't know the person who left us. It all helps.

And then, one day, it doesn't hurt as much anymore. There are fewer tears. The heartache is a slight pang, no longer a life-threatening lightning bolt-sized panic in the middle of the night.

It took me years and a ton of different forms of therapy to finally realize that Robby's death had nothing to do with me. He was battling something so profound inside himself that he didn't know how to talk about it, much less handle it. To him, it was insurmountable, so he did what he thought was best for everyone who was left behind. But, man, did he get that one wrong!

My dad loved Robby and thought the world of him. When I heard about Robby, Dad was the second person I called, followed by my cousin Derek, to make sure Robby was protected until the police could take over.

I didn't trust some of the people in our community not to rob us blind. Allan and John were dealing with that situation alone and needed help ASAP. My dad told me not to worry. He would do whatever I needed him to do.

New Beginnings

"Just get home safe, please. I don't need to lose another one of my family." Later, my dad told me that Robby had called him a couple of times earlier to say he was calling to see how he was. But Dad has always felt like there was something more, and he was now feeling guilty because he didn't see it as clearly as he saw it later. But no one had. No one ever saw this coming. He hid it well.

Several of our friends will forever have a picture of that morning seared into their minds, as well as the aftermath of how it all unfolded. Dana, my lifelong best friend, saw things that a friend should never have to see as they lifted Robby off the ground to place him on the gurney to transport his remains to the funeral home. She later told me that she had nightmares for months and was so grateful it was her instead of me.

When she heard the news, she worked at Lizana Elementary School, where we met Robby for the first time in fourth grade. Dana is a first-grade teacher there, and Derek's wife had come to tell her what had happened to Robby. Dana just got up and left, thinking I was home alone. She didn't hesitate to get to and be beside me, not realizing I wasn't even there. She also had no qualms about protecting my husband's remains from onlookers, even though doing so would cause her harm later.

Dana was at my house many times over the next few weeks, bringing me food, checking on me, and making sure I wasn't spending holidays alone—the kinds of things your heavenly twin and lifelong bestie would do without thinking about it to ensure you were still breathing the same air they were.

Jay, a business colleague, had become such a vital part of my life as a colleague and friend that when life started again for me with Jay, he too had begun to find time for a new relationship: one that would finally mean he would have a lifelong partner and wife. Still, fate took over, and that wasn't a reality.

When Jay and I started seeing one another, it came with more lies and rumors from Robby's girls and his mother, which led me to believe that the source of the gossip came from his youngest daughter and possibly his ex-wife. Jay took me out for my birthday dinner, but not on an actual date. But before I agreed, I went to see Robby's mom for permission. I didn't need to do it but felt I owed it to her. I still looked up to her, and she was still my mother-in-law. And because no other relative lived near us, I still looked after her when her caregiver was gone.

As fate would have it, Jay and I were on the same page, not realizing it. Still, we were both wanting to end the relationship, and on Valentine's Day 2019, Jay and I were about to go over to visit Robby's mom when he got the news that he had stage-4 lymphoma and was also battling bone cancer. So, our differences were put on the back burner, and life-battling illnesses just kept hitting him and trying to win the battle. After four and a half years, he was in remission from 4th cancer. We got a call that nearly took him out altogether: his mom, Helen, had passed away. We had just lost her boyfriend and childhood friend, BB. BB had been in love with her since they were teenagers, but nothing happened because Jay's dad, Kenneth, stole her heart and moved her away.

When Jay went into remission, he became someone I didn't recognize. His anger would come out of nowhere. When I researched this trait in cancer patients, I found out that chemo changes personality and chemistry as well.

I called my oldest son one afternoon, and unbeknownst to me, he was texting his brother when we were talking. I told him that Jay and I had just broken up and why, which I later regretted deeply. I hadn't realized the depths that

Robby's death had affected my boys or even the other family members who dropped their lives to come running to protect me that week. Even though Dana almost lost her job for leaving her class to get me (not realizing I was not even in town at the time) and Derek and Michelle dropped their lives to watch over Robby's body with Dana until the police and coroner could survive, it hadn't yet hit me how Robby's death affected them.

Six hours away in Houston, lives were shattered, too. Ronnie and B drove together to get to me, and her husband, David, drove six hours to help my boys and dad build a memorial where Robby took his life so that people would not walk over it or park their cars when they came to offer their condolences. Diana and Caesar drove from Houston just to help cook and clean. Brock had to find Jim for me. When Jim heard about it, he was at work and broke down. When he returned to work on Monday, he got laid off for leaving the job site. Jim, Tifeni, and my two grandsons drove all night to get to me the following day. None of them left my side all week.

Ronnie was locking the gate by 3:00 p.m. Dana had to explain to me that all of these people who had personally sacrificed to be with me were the ones who would be making sure I was okay when everyone went back to their lives that next week— "So, don't shut them out," she warned. "Your momma will need them when you and Jim have to go home."

Back to me breaking up with Jay. When Jim heard what happened with Jay and me, he went into protective mode and said some harsh things to Jay. I had to tell Jim that he needed to stop and hear the whole story before he lashed out. Ultimately, he and Jay shared their thoughts and feelings on the matter, but no love was lost for either my boys or Jay. Life as a cancer patient's caregiver was a hard one, plus running a business, trying to survive, and still grieving my husband's death. Taking care of myself was hard and unhealthy at times.

Then Covid hit. Because Jay was a cancer patient, I felt pressured to change how warm I was to everyone. This caused my boys to resent Jay even more than they formerly had. They saw how Jay allowed his family to come and go whenever they wanted, but there were restrictions for my family. Later, when we split for good, I learned that the root cause of our problems was that living in a house he didn't own wouldn't provide me with the most basic kinds of support. He felt that because he had no say, he would control what he could, which was his visitors.

In the end, I had to say, "Enough. My whole family is always welcome here, and so is yours. To me, they are all my family." Ultimately, his son and daughter-in-law continued to reach out to me. His grandbabies have been to my home several times to spend time with me on school holidays, just like they did when we were together.

I started spending more time in Houston when Jay and I ended it. My boys have always called me for advice, but now I was calling them because I felt I had no one to confide in. I was lost. My dad was always there, but he is getting up in age and can't hear very well, so he gets frustrated when he can't understand what I'm saying. So I call my boys more now. They have helped me work through my vehicle situations, helping me decide what I should or shouldn't have.

I didn't ask for their advice when it came to keeping a truck that I loved (the cost of diesel had gone through the roof). I traded it because another man (I believe) had felt inferior for my driving a nicer, paid-off large truck that I felt safe in and for which he had nothing to do with other than drive it when in town. He talked me

New Beginnings

into trading it for a smaller truck that was gas, not diesel, and I ended up losing money on the car.

Another life lesson: trust yourself and your gut. It is okay to hear other opinions but hear your own first. Ask those who have your best interest at heart— not those who feel the need to make you feel less than they are.

In the end, my boys have always been my biggest fan. Ronnie always says, "Momma, I wish you could see the Momma I see." Until he left the Navy, he would come flying in the back door and call out, "Momma, I'm home!" That would always make me smile.

Robby and I had gone to his Naval Graduation in Chicago. When he first saw me, he would say, "This is my Momma," as if I were the only one on the planet with that title. Jim once told me that being able to say "Momma" and knowing I would be there made him feel safe. He said that the weekly letters we wrote to him while he was at Parris Island, Marine Corp boot camp, made him feel that he was never alone and that those thirteen letters are what got him through the sand pit visits, the yelling, and all the screaming they made him go through. When he saw me just before his boot camp graduation, I cried. He had lost so much weight. He held me tight and said, "Momma, do not cry. I am like my grandpa now. I am a Marine."

Like every parent, I have made some mistakes in my parenting years. Still, they have always forgiven me and loved me as I do them, without malice, judgment, or expectations other than true love.

A girl's first true love is indeed her daddy. But when she gives birth to sons, it's hard to believe that there is enough love in such a tiny little vessel in her body that can love so big. Yes, it hurts over the years as they grow up, move on, have lives and kids of their own, and bring home the daughters that mommas didn't have to spend teenage years fighting with. Still, mine gave me Tifeni, a beautiful new look on life. We have our misunderstandings, too, but there is no one like her. She showed up the week of Robby's death and took control of the kitchen, cooked and cleaned for everyone, and still knew where her babies were at all times. She sent me photos of my grandsons waving and blowing kisses. I talked to Wyatt one afternoon on FaceTime, and she took a picture of him. He had parked himself in the hallway and was chatting it up with his Nana as if nothing else mattered in the world but him and me.

My grandbabies each have a special place in

my heart. Wyatt once told me his heart hurt because he loved her more when he was with his MeeMaw. When he was with me, he loved me more. I had to explain to him that it didn't matter who he loved more because his tiny little heart could handle it, and there was plenty more love there for everyone else.

Benjamin is a complex little one. On the one hand, he is the image of his dad's emotions with the warm heart to help others in need. On the other, he has his Uncle Ronnie's insight on certain things. He wants to have Nana sleepovers every night when I am in Houston, which makes his little world just as it should be. I once stayed the night with them the day before leaving to return home. I said my goodbyes the night before, but I snuck out before everyone woke up, and little Ben woke up to me not being there. He became inconsolable, and even though I was more than two hours away by then, I turned around and went right back to make sure he was good and stayed another night.

Baby Jerry, named after my dad, is the funny one. What an imagination he has. He loves to pretend to be a chef. From the moment he could stand up, he loved to watch cooking shows and bring me his creations from his make-believe kitchen. I told him I would see him on TV at one of those cooking competitions.

And now, seven years later, we have Zachary Morgan, such a sweet, calm, tender little week-old baby boy. He fits so perfectly in the middle of my chest. We cannot wait to see his personality come to life. Tifeni, the amazing daughter-in-law and momma that she is, has put a no-vacancy sign on her uterus. Four little boys are enough to help her and Jim fight the zombies.

But the love between a momma and her sons is unwavering, even when they do not see eye to eye. My boys played, and still do, a massive part in my survival over the last seven years. I get texts saying Love You, Mom, or Have a great day, Mom, and they get them in return, too. I know that all I have to do is say I need y'all.

My trips to Houston have been less frequent lately. With me closing our business, I had to become an employee and now must punch the clock. This is taking some getting used to and is something other than what I like. I keep telling myself, "This, too, shall pass." It is just another life lesson that I have had to make since Robby's death, but my boys know I am right there if they need me.

Jay and I ended our relationship three weeks after the last split. In four years, I went from colleague to girlfriend to caregiver to fiancé, even though the caregiver role never transitioned into the girlfriend role. In the end, Jay could not "see" me as being anyone but his caretaker, and the anger he vented while dealing with his chemo brain was just too much for me. The toll that our relationship experienced was just too much for any couple to bear—one that was already rocky and destined for failure. It was just a matter of time.

I went on a couple of dates and had a very short relationship with someone I grew up with. But we said goodbye, and it was yet another lesson learned that I added to my long list of life's lessons. I have always said it is not a mistake if you walk away learning something. There had been another attempt, but this one was filled with lies, deceptions, and harmful fantasies that I could not even imagine. I called it quits on Thanksgiving after I was cussed at and told to use some common sense when a boiled egg rolled off the chopping board and onto the floor, all while he just sat back and watched.

December 22, 2022, started as just another day. Because my best friend, Natalie, kept telling me about finding a good man I could trust, I joined a dating site and set up my profile. Before completing my profile, I had already gotten my first wink from Bill, a very handsome, distinguished man.

Bill was a retired Police Chief from Baxter Springs, Kansas, who lived on a sailboat in Slidell, Louisiana. It had been twenty-plus years since I had stepped aboard a sailboat, much less skippered one. Does your brain recall all the information after all that time, or is it something that must be relearned? I guess we will find out. Do we even want to find out at this age?

Bill was among my top ten picks, so I looked at his profile closely. I studied his eyes, the most beautiful shade of steel blue that captivated my soul. It was like I had met him in another life or something. Is that even possible? He looked familiar to me, even more than Robby did after twenty-two years of not seeing him before we re-met.

And then it happened. On December 23rd, he sent me a private message, and that was all it took. We sent messages all day, and on the 23rd and 24th of Christmas Eve, at 6:00 a.m., he sent me a message.

Good morning, Beautiful.

It was like my heart was coming alive, and I was that teenage girl again, waiting for that one guy to ask me out, to notice me, and to hear me.

Within an hour, he messaged me again while I was baking pies for Christmas.

This is getting hard. Can we please exchange numbers?

OH MY, he wants to have my number! I texted Natalie, and all she said was, *and… LOL.*

Bill and I exchanged numbers, texting like crazed teenagers until about 3:00 p.m. when he finally sent me the following message.

You can call me if you like.

Within seconds of me saying the same thing, he called me. His voice was so calming. It was as if God and Robby had gotten together, heard all my prayers, and created this man that I was so drawn to I couldn't wait to hear his voice again. I felt that I could not live another moment without him.

We talked until I had to get dressed for Mass with my mom, but I called him the second I got back home, and we talked for hours again. On Christmas Day, I woke up to a text from him.

Good morning, beautiful.

Once we started talking, we realized that he and my boys' father were stationed at Fort Carson, Colorado, at the same time. So, our little inside joke is that we met on "Aisle 27" at the base commissary.

✦✦✦

My seventeen-year stay in Gulfport, Mississippi, has been nothing but lessons learned. I am still praying that there is hope for a forever kind of love for me that will last until the good Lord calls one of us home.

And so the circle of life begins again.

-------------**STAKE IT!**-------------

QUESTION: *On a scale of 1 to 5, how much of your self-worth, needs, and concerns do you feel are allowed to be expressed in your current relationship?*

CONSIDERATION: During the loss of a partner, the power of dreams is a guiding light, shining a pathway of hope and possibility in the middle of challenging circumstances. Much like surveying uncharted territory, you must harness the power of your dreams to envision a brighter future, even in the wake of loss or adversity. Coping with loss requires resilience and strength, as you navigate the emotional upheaval and grief that come with losing a partner.

Navigating work challenges requires adaptability and perseverance to overcome obstacles and complete (or achieve) professional goals in the middle of personal turmoil.

Finding love again can offer you the opportunity to forge new connections and experiences, restoring hope and excitement to your romantic landscape.

Learning lessons from past experiences serves as invaluable insight, guiding you towards healthier relationships and informed decision-making.

So, by embracing the transformational power of dreams, navigating loss and work challenges with resilience, finding new love, and learning from past experiences, you can navigate loss with some level of courage, forging pathways towards healing, growth, and eventual fulfillment.

CHALLENGE: If you are still with your partner, let them know how much you love them! If you aren't with your partner due to a break-up or death, I pray that you receive the peace and grace of God to get through today and tomorrow until you experience the hope of having a new adventure.

The day of Robby's memorial: BOTTOM LEFT: Shelley, my rock that day and the one who drove me home. BOTTOM RIGHT: Barbie 'B,' my ex-sister-in-law, but we kept our ex-husbands' mother in the divorce. LEFT: Me. RIGHT TOP: Selma, my best friend and John's wife. LEFT TOP: Dana, my lifelong best friend. BACK: John, my brother from another mother (and mister), the one who found Robby that morning. Grateful for this circle of love.

Special Acknowledgments

I want to offer a special memory to those who have passed since I began drafting this book and who held a special place in my heart.

Uncle Tom Grozan passed away unexpectedly on January 1, 2024. He married my Aunt Debbie when they were just out of college. He was always an amazing, quiet, loving, and funny man who had no idea how much I loved him.

Nicole Dees passed suddenly on March 12, 2024. We had our little issues, but even so, there was always laughter and her crazy jokes every time we talked. Just the day before she passed, we laughed and shared stories about our usual crazy lives. She told me she had a feeling that this was our year for beautiful things to happen to us both. She got the last laugh because now she gets to live a most beautiful and peaceful life every day.

Mrs. Nadine Nichols, June 9, 2024, was my cheerleading coach for sixth, seventh, and eighth grades. She was always such an inspiration to every child who had the privilege of knowing her. We have so many beautiful memories around her, but I had the honor of having her input on this book. She never got to see the final draft, but she told me the following before she passed: "I know that it will be great because it is coming from your heart."

QUESTIONS
For Book Discussion

Discussion #1

1. How do I handle the immediate aftermath of my partner's passing?

2. What legal steps should I take following his death?

3. How do I manage finances and access important documents?

Discussion #2

4. Are there any life insurance policies or benefits I should be aware of?

5. What support systems are available to me in terms of friends, family, or support groups?

6. How can I address grief and take care of my mental health?

Discussion #3

7. What are the funeral and memorial service arrangements that need to be made?

8. Are there any outstanding debts or financial obligations to consider?

9. How do I navigate the probate process?

Discussion #4

10. What resources are available for counseling and emotional support?

11. How can I communicate the news to children or other family members?

12. What changes should I make to my living arrangements, if any?

Discussion #5

13. Are there social security benefits or other government assistance programs for widows?

14. How can I handle practical aspects like canceling subscriptions or changing account information?

15. What are the steps for updating legal documents like wills and beneficiaries?

Discussion #6

16. How do I address the legalities of property and assets?

17. Are there any memorial or legacy projects I might consider?

18. How can I cope with the loneliness and isolation that may follow?

Discussion #7

19. What steps can I take to manage stress and maintain physical health?

20. How do I handle the process of notifying friends and extended family?

21. Are there legal implications for joint accounts and shared property?

Discussion #8

22. What are the options for childcare or support if I have children?

23. How can I navigate the emotions of moving forward while honoring my late husband's memory?

24. What are the potential tax implications or benefits to be aware of?

Discussion #9

25. How do I handle social interactions and questions from others about my husband's passing?

26. Are there specific legal or financial professionals I should consult for guidance?

27. How can I preserve and share memories of my husband with others?

Discussion #10

28. What are the potential challenges in dealing with family dynamics during this time?

29. How do I approach the division of personal items and belongings?

30. Are there financial planning considerations for the long term?

Discussion #11

31. How can I establish a support network for ongoing assistance?

32. What steps should I take regarding my late husband's online presence and accounts?

33. How do I address the emotional impact on children or teenagers?

Discussion #12

34. Are there estate planning considerations I should be aware of?

35. What are the key aspects of self-care during this period?

36. How can I navigate potential legal disputes or challenges?

Discussion #13

37. What are the options for creating a memorial or tribute to my late husband?

38. How do I manage the practical aspects of day-to-day life during the grieving process?

39. Are there financial or legal pitfalls I should be cautious of?

Discussion #14

40. How can I balance honoring my late husband's memory while moving forward with my own life?

41. What are the potential challenges in returning to work or daily routines?

42. How can I address questions from acquaintances or colleagues about my husband's passing?

Discussion #15

43. Are there resources for continuing education or career support?

44. What are the potential emotional triggers, and how can I cope with them?

45. How do I handle the legal aspects of any ongoing businesses or joint ventures?

46. What steps can I take to create a positive and supportive living environment?

Discussion #16

47. How can I navigate social events or gatherings after the loss?

48. What are the potential impacts on my own health, both physical and mental?

49. How can I find meaning and purpose in life after the loss?

50. Are there legal considerations related to social security benefits or pensions?

LEFT: Benjamin, my little car -ixing artist. RIGHT: Wyatt loves science and video games. BOTTOM: Jerry, our future Top Chef champion . They are what keeps me going even though they are six hours away. Their dad or mom will call me and the boys will yell out, "Love you, Nana!" What a day that makes!

Photo
Gallery

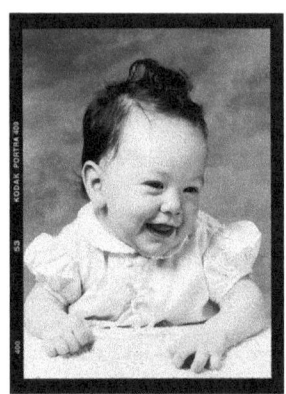

UPPER LEFT: Me at six months old in Gulfport, Mississippi, around the time of my christening at St. Anne's Catholic Church in Lizana, Mississippi. UPPER RIGHT: My brothers, Danny, Michael, and me. I'm about two, at my paternal grandparents' house, Probably Sunday mass and probably before my father left for Vietnam. BOTTOM: At Camp Lejeune. A family Christmas portrait the just before my father shipped out to Vietnam.

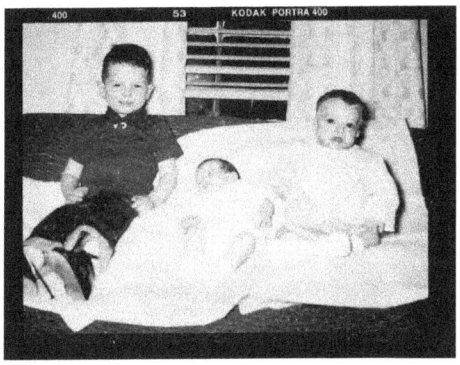

UPPER LEFT: My father in Vietnam. UPPER RIGHT:: My paternal grandmother BOTTOM (from left to right): My brothers Michael, Danny, and my brother Jason who passed away at two years of age.

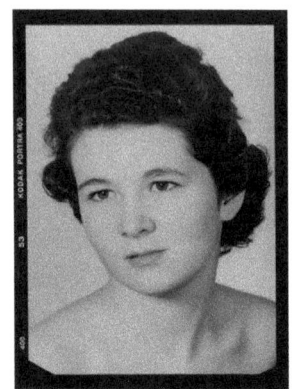

UPPER LEFT: Julia, my aunt who raised me ("My Momma") in her senior portrait. UPPER RIGHT: My NanNan in her eighth-grade portrait. BOTTOM: Me with my Paw Paw, Fred Right, and Granny Etha Mae.

TOP: Fourth-grade Valentine's Day Court. Me with Rodney.
BOTTOM LEFT: Me in my 7th-grade basketball uniform.
BOTTOM RIGHT: Me in my sophomore school photo in Pasadena, Texas.

UPPER LEFT: My dad and me in 2023.
UPPER RIGHT: My sister-in-law "B" and me.
BOTTOM LEFT: My friend Selma and me after Robby's death
BOTTOM RIGHT: My friend Monica and me.

About the Author

In Through Widow's Eyes: What Happens after Suicide, *Tammie Osborne pulls back the curtain on the darkest chapter of her life, navigating readers through the heart-wrenching aftermath of her husband's tragic suicide, the likely consequence of a devastating business deal that became his final straw.*

Reflecting on her almost decade-long battle with the aftermath, Tammie exposes raw, uncomfortable truths and shares vital principles and lessons she wished she had learned before tragedy struck. Skillfully weaving between past and present, she offers an intimate portrayal of the highs and lows of her early life, highlights circumstances that led her to marry the love of her life, and explores the personal and societal pressures that contributed to her husband's despair and final act.

But this poignant memoir is not just a chronicle of grief: it's a beacon of resilience as Tammie learns to make sense of the senseless in micro-stages that, in retrospect, offers a roadmap for readers who might be experiencing similar situations.

Tammie Osborne's memoir invites readers to confront their own shadows, find hope and healing, and discover the courage to face life's challenges. In short, Through Widow's Eyes: What Happens after Suicide *is a testament to the strength of the human spirit.*

Traitmarker Media
www.traitmarkermedia.com
traitmarker@gmail.com

www.ingramcontent.com/pod-product-compliance
Lightning Source LLC
LaVergne TN
LVHW052047070526
838201LV00087B/5249